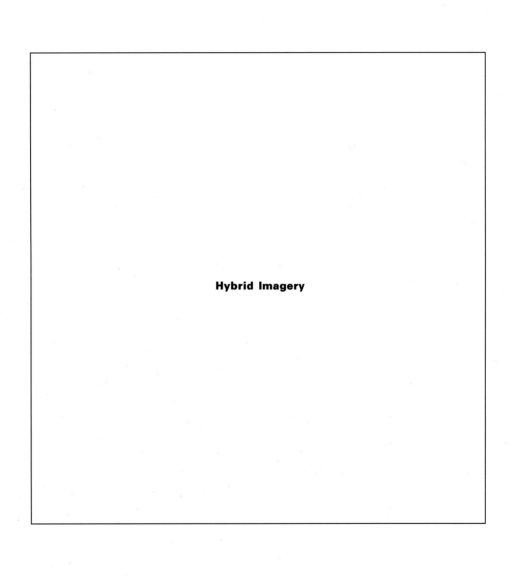

Hybrid Imagery

A picture is not worked out
in advance. It changes whil
ing on it, keeping pace wi
And when it's finished it
changing, depending on the
son who happens to be looki
picture has its own life l
creature. It undergoes the
all undergo in daily life.
natural, because the pictur
so long as people look at

—— **Picasso**

completely
you are work-
ill keeps on
od of the per-
g at it. A
e a living
ame changes we
his is quite
is only alive

The fusion of technology and graphic design

Hybrid Imagery

with overviews by Eric Martin

April Greiman

Architecture Design and Technology Press/London

First published in Great Britain 1990 by
Architecture Design and Technology Press
128 Long Acre
London
WC2E 9AN
(a Division of Longman Group UK Limited)

ISBN 1 85454 354 7

Printed in Singapore

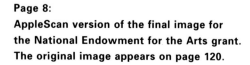

Page 8:
AppleScan version of the final image for
the National Endowment for the Arts grant.
The original image appears on page 120.

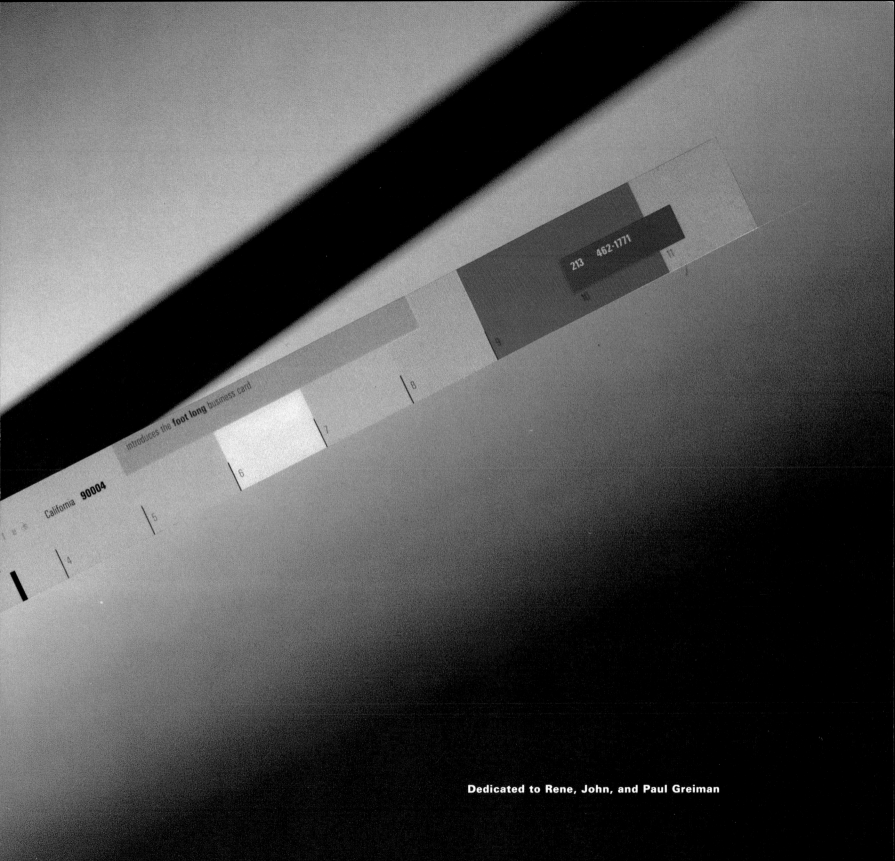

Dedicated to Rene, John, and Paul Greiman

Contents

The meaning of the word "implode" is "to burst inward." This definition captures the spirit and dynamic of the digital revolution and its profound impact on existing disciplines, graphic design among them. I say "among them" advisedly, since the broad effect of this revolution is to bring many things much closer than they have been since the industrial revolution made specialists of us all: idea and realization, producer and client, creation and revision, word / image / sound / movement. In short, digital technology is no respecter of existing boundaries, whether spatial, temporal, conceptual, or professional. ▶

▼

Similarly, "primitive" cultures, whether ancient or contemporary, see no need to distinguish between art, science, and religion when considering an act, a thought, or an object. In their view, these are all aspects of a common meaning. As April Greiman's work illustrates, the natural bias of the new digital language is to bring processes which had become isolated into a common weave. And so the use of the word "hybrid" in the title of this book is intended to suggest a reintegration not only of media but of the act of design as a whole. ■

—— Eric Martin

"There is no resistance unless there is movement"
AG

> "IT TAKES AWHILE BEFORE YOU CAN STEP OVER INERT BODIES
>
> AND GO AHEAD WITH WHAT YOU WERE WANTING TO DO."
>
> —— **Jenny Holzer**

The Layering Process

Casual / Formal

East / West

Male / Female

Intuition / Reason

Motion / Stasis

Unity / Diversity

Dream / Waking

Tribal / Electronic

New Wave / No Wave

April Greiman's approach questions the conventional idea that dualities are opposed pairs. Instead she suggests that they are interdependent possibilities at play in a common field. Her broader themes—the constancy of change, form as energy, and the interconnectedness of matter in space and time—take this approach to its limits. Nowhere is this more apparent than in the increasing variety of sources and techniques she incorporates into her images.

From her earliest published works, spontaneity and conscious precision collaborate to define a unique personal landscape. This play of opposites also has an effect within her profession, which is suffering a profound identity crisis as a consequence of a sudden technological revolution. For many, the replacement of photomechanical methods by electronic processes threatens the very standards of the profession. In Greiman's case, these new tools extend new opportunity to the traditional relationship between hand and eye.

This is not a "how to" book in the literal sense of that term. How can it be, when a method described on page 50 is obsolete by the time you get to page 100? The pace of technological change today is literally electric—the million-dollar graphic workstation of yesterday is the affordable personal computer of today.

In other words, the purpose of this book is to express an underlying attitude, to show how a variety of technologies may be woven together to express a common vision, a unity within diversity which is particularly contemporary. The principle is universal; not "either / or" but "yes, and."

The computer collapses all conventional media into a common digital language of patterns of on / off electrical impulses. The boundaries between previously separate formats and skills begin to blur. Greiman has coined the term "hybrid imagery" to describe this mingling of digital image / text / page composition technology with traditional photomechanical techniques for print production. In fact, her work from the beginning has had this hybrid aspect in its layering of a classical feel for typography, which derives from her Swiss training, with the freedom and energy of her southern California environment.

This layering took on an added complexity in the early 1980s with the inclusion of video imagery (the "STA" and "Ron Rezek" posters). Her discovery of the Macintosh computer in 1984 added digital technology to the mix, and most recently her access to highly sophisticated electronic graphic systems has further extended her reach.

The incorporation of new technology began as an adjunct to conventional print production. Lately, however, it has enabled Greiman to work in a number of formats: outdoor sculpture (the "Pacific Wave" piece for the Fortuny Museum, Venice, Italy), architectural tile patterns (the Cerritos Theatre project), and environmental signage (several clients).

Where all this will lead is, of course, anybody's guess. Digital technology is entering a period in which it is not only reinventing print technology but is creating wholly new formats which combine sound, motion, and interactivity. These new digital hybrids will become the platform for the designers of tomorrow.

The revolution continues. — EM

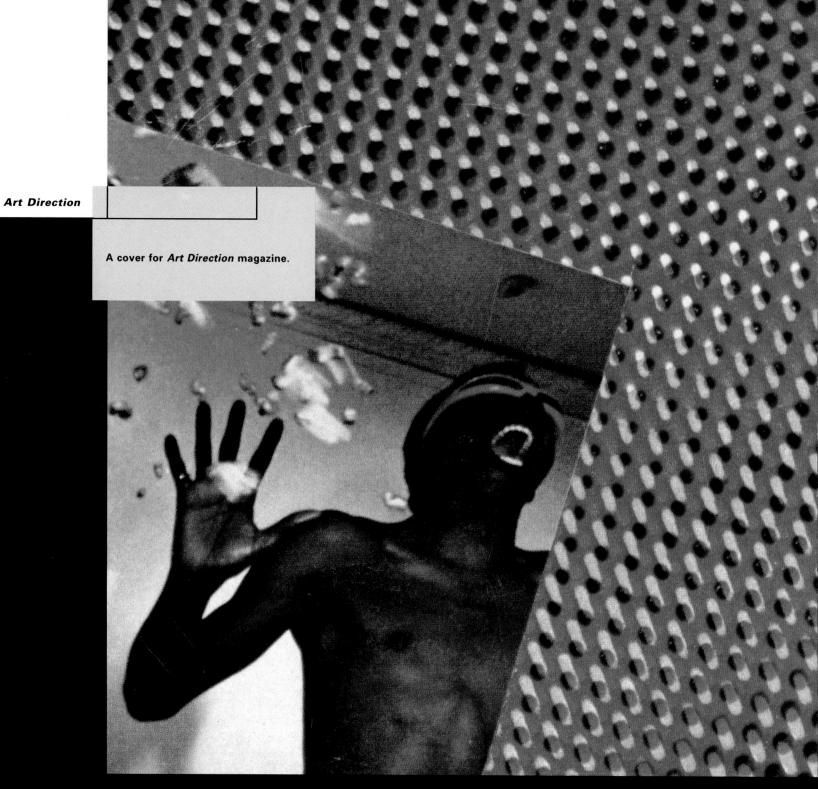

Art Direction

A cover for *Art Direction* magazine.

Detail of color Xerox

The Magazine
of Visual Communica
July 1978
$1.75

Art Direction

This early cover is

an example of my use

of hybrid techniques

well before electronic

imagery entered the

studio. The typography

plays off a collage of

a color Xerox of a blown

up printer's gradation

and a color photograph

of dancers. The black-

and-white gradation

acquired color through

the color Xerox process

prior to the paste-up,

helping to create one

graphic / photographic

environment.

Peter Shire

Collaboration with Jayme Odgers

A poster and advertisements for the designer, Peter Shire.

This combination of a Western and Japanese sense of space caused this poster to be referred to in the studio as "Swissiyaki." A photograph of a corner of a room was collaged with cutout found imagery, cut and pasted type, colored punched paper, a photograph of the designer, calligraphy, and ink splotches. The composite, including proofs of the type, was then photographed as a single image and reproduced in two-color offset (black and yellow). In this poster, the type is literally "in" the image.

The "bamboo" portion of the black plate was scraped by the press foreman to purify the appearance of yellow in the bamboo stalk itself. The Day-Glo red-orange color required a single additional pass in silk screen.

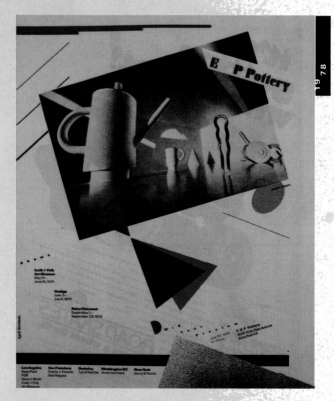

Two-color ad in *WET* magazine

The completed poster

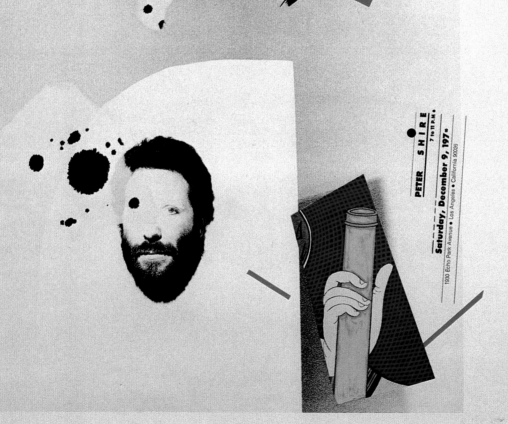

Two-color and three-color versions of an ad

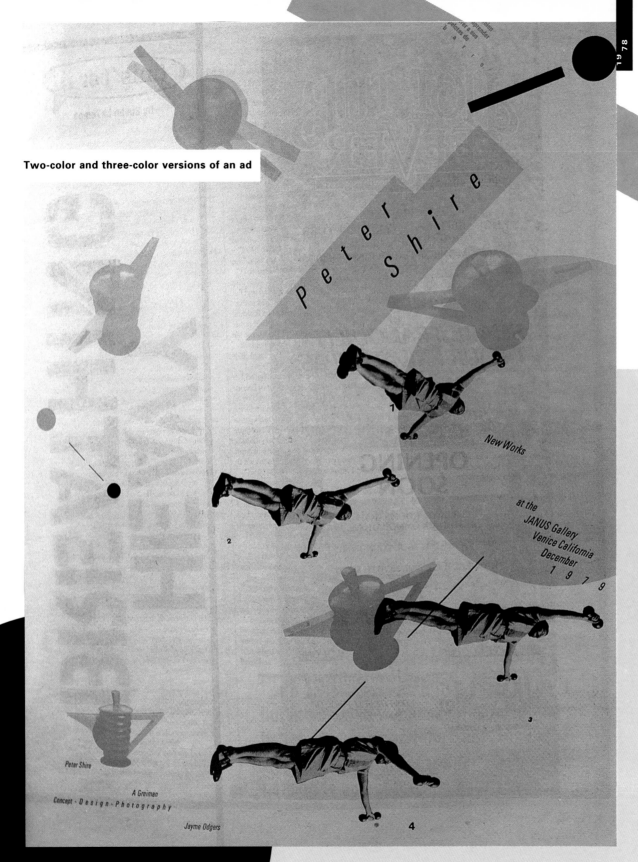

Peter Shire

New Works

at the
JANUS Gallery
Venice California
December
1 9 7 9

Peter Shire

A Greiman
Concept · Design · Photography

Jayme Odgers

Two-color ad in *WET* magazine

Three-color ad in *Stuff* magazine

An identity,

cards,

and sign

for a

clothing,

accessories,

magazine,

and gift store

on the

Melrose strip

in Los Angeles.

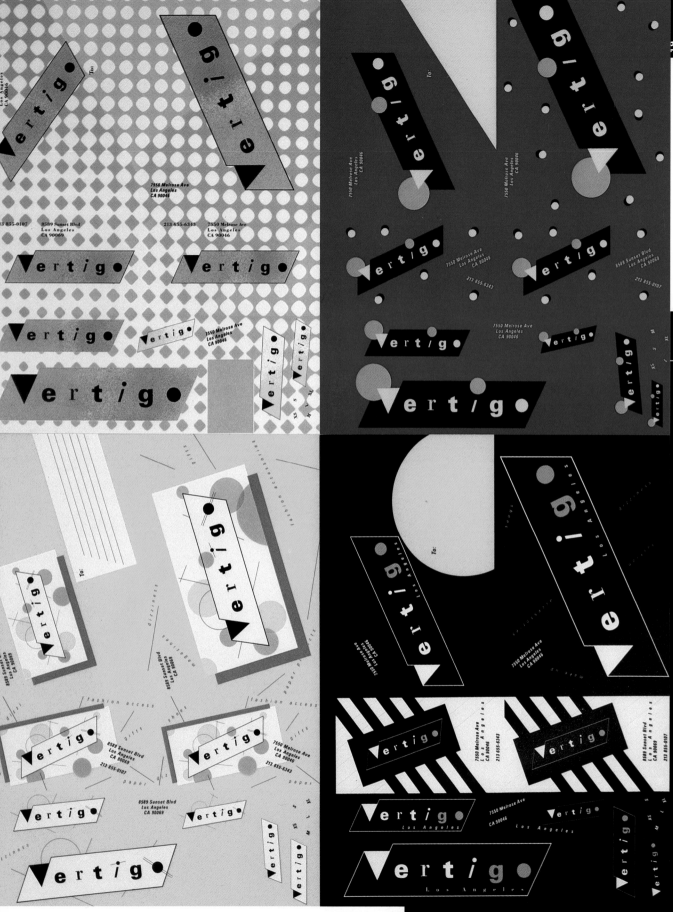

A family of

business cards,

postcards,

and hang

tags were

trimmed out

of a single

poster-sized

sheet containing

variations on

the basic

"Vertigo" logotype.

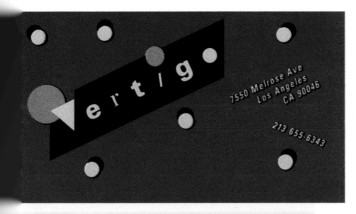

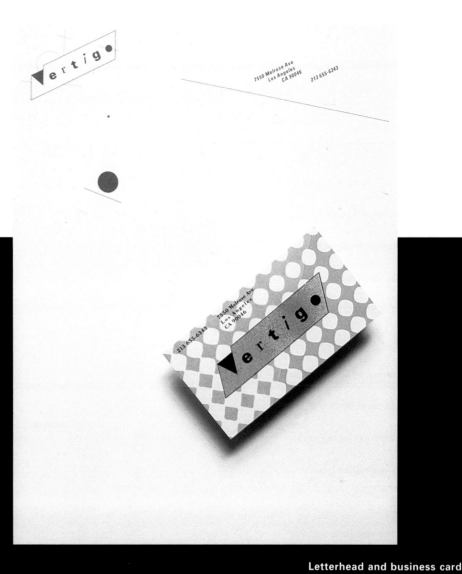

Letterhead and business card

One of four variations on the logotype

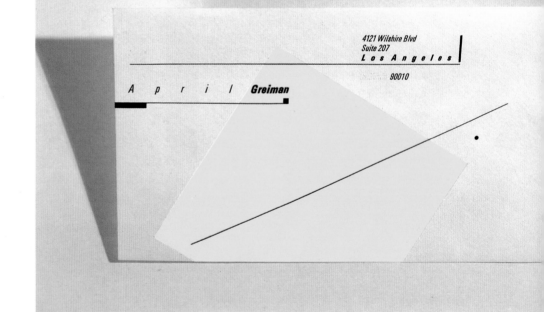

April Greiman, Inc.

Letterheads for April Greiman, Inc.

These letterheads express my design evolution succinctly. Produced in 1979, 1981, and 1982, this series shows my first conscious use of basic shapes as universal symbols: the yellow square represents earth; the green triangle stands for fire, and also the dynamic nature of a triad; the embossed oval represents holism and the self.

1979

A p r i l **Greiman**

4121 Wilshire Blvd
Suite 207
L o s A n g e l e s

90010

213 3 8 3 - 0 9 0 4

A p r i l **Greiman**

4121 Wilshire Blvd
Suite 207
L o s A n g e l e s

90010

April Greiman
301 N Gower **L o s A n g e l e s**
California **90004**

213 / 462-1771

Type is used

to create

a landscape

in space.

W

E

S

April Greiman
April Greiman
Incorporated

213   227-1222

620 Moulton Avenue

Los Angeles

California 90031

#211

19 82

Signage and dinner plate

The China Club

A complete visual identity for
a popular Los Angeles restaurant

and lounge, including logotype,
menu, exterior sign, advertisements,
and interior elements.

Two-color ad

used prior to

club opening

Etched backlit mirror inside restaurant

Four-color ad

"T"- time ad

Wine list

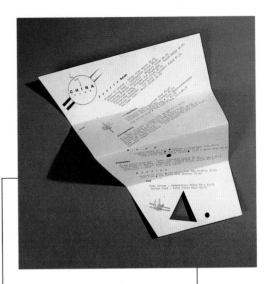

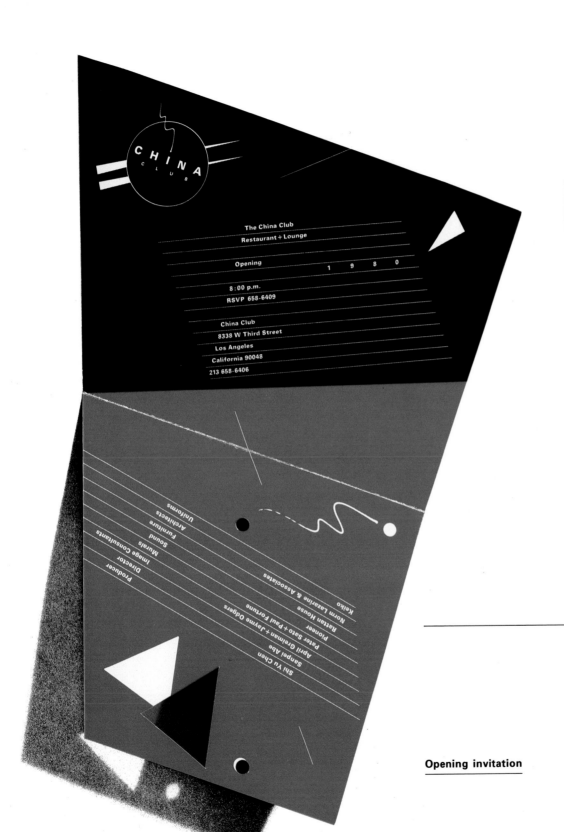

Ingenuity was required

to extend the design as fully

as possible. For example,

the die plate for the eccentric

silhouette of the invitation,

easily the most expensive

part of this application, was

reused for the inexpensive

take-out menu, which was

set on a typewriter.

Opening invitation

WET

Collaboration with Jayme Odgers

A cover for an issue of *WET* magazine ("The Magazine of Gourmet Bathing"), which epitomized New Wave Los Angeles culture of the mid-to-late 1970s.

A color Xerox of a photograph of Ricky Nelson was combined with Japanese papers, cutouts from magazines, and airbrushing. The entire handmade collage was then photographed as a single image for four-color separation as the cover.

Douglas Schmidt

Collaboration with Jayme Odgers

A moving announcement (poster) for the set designer, Douglas Schmidt.

This composition was produced as a layered series of stages. The first, or background, layer began as a collage birthday card from me to Odgers, its surface altered by the addition of paint splatters, clock numerals, and a cutout photo of the Paramount Building (Schmidt's new location). Photographs and other elements were positioned above the collage surface (with their cast shadows), and then photographed in color as a single composite image.

Additional elements were added to a Cibachrome color print of the photograph and the whole rephotographed as a single image by the printer for four-color offset reproduction. An additional pass in Day-Glo ink added the yellow-orange palette shape. The trapezoidal shape of the poster was die cut.

The completed poster

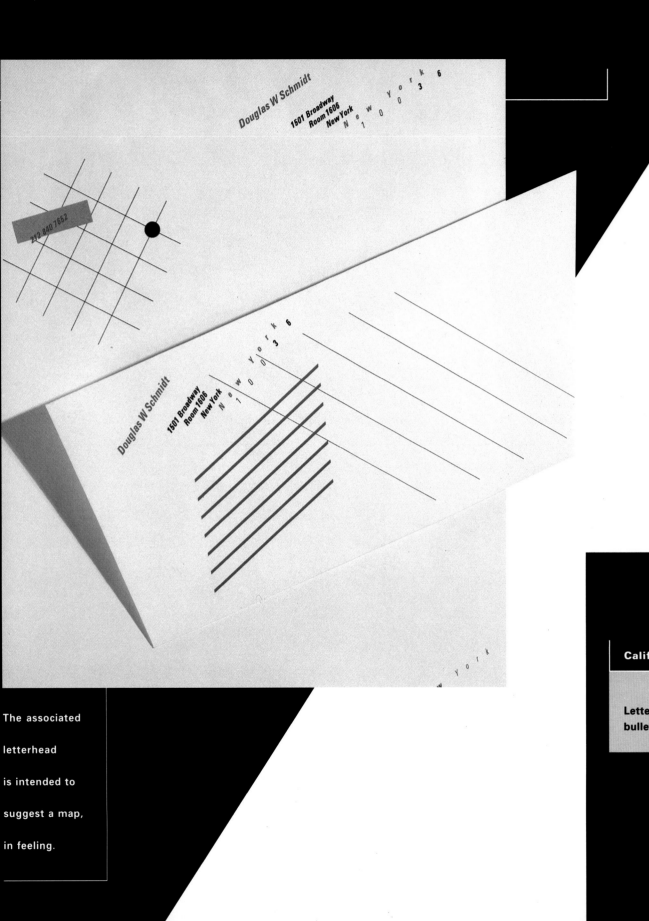

Douglas W Schmidt
1501 Broadway
Room 1606
New York
New York
1 0 0 3 6

212 840 7652

Douglas W Schmidt
1501 Broadway
Room 1606
New York
New York
1 0 0 3 6

New York

The associated

letterhead

is intended to

suggest a map,

in feeling.

California Institute of the Arts

**Letterhead, posters, admissions
bulletins, and viewbook for CalArts.**

California Institute of the Arts

My association with CalArts encompassed five years and many formats, examples of which have come to stand for New Wave graphic design in California in the 1970s and early 1980s.

The wide CalArts poster / mailer project combined the photographic concept and execution of Jayme Odgers with typographic design by me. The hybrid nature of the image is meant to suggest the hybrid nature of CalArts, which instructs in all the arts, separately and in combination.

1979

CAL ART IS VIEW

MUSIC

DANCE

California Institute of the Arts

ART+DESIGN

FILM+VIDEO

THEATRE

Black-and-white interior
pages integrate type, black
shapes, and photography
into a single active landscape.

The CalArts Viewbook is a
tabloid-size overview of
CalArts, printed on newsprint.

FILM + VIDEO

School of Film and Video

Located near the film and television capital
of the world, the School of Film and Video
offers students experience in a wide
spectrum of technical and artistic activities.
Introductory courses train students in the
technology and craft of film and video.
Subsequent work emphasizes projects
developed by individual students, with
faculty guidance and supervision, inde-
pendent collaboration with a variety of
artists from the other Schools at CalArts —
musicians, composers, dancers, actors
and visual artists — is not only possible,
but usual.

The School of Film and Video has three
major programs, Live Action Film and
Video, Film Graphics and Character Animation. Students are accepted to application to the Live Action program in February 1st. The Character Animation and Film
Graphics programs' deadlines are April 1,
however enrollment is limited and appli-
cants are urged to apply before the end
of March.

Character Animation (B.F.A., Certificate)
The Character Animation program is highly
structured study of full animation in the
classic style. The curriculum was designed
in consultation with artists and executives
of Walt Disney Studios. Subjects studied
include life drawing, color, design, kinetic
figure studies and the technology of animation. Admission to the program is based on
a portfolio. Samples of an applicant's quick
sketches in pen or pencil of human's and
animals in action is most useful to the
evaluation committee. Prior experience in
filmmaking or animation is not required for
students in Character Animation.

Live Action Film and Video
(M.F.A., B.F.A., Certificate)
All new students in Live Action Film and
Video participate in the Basic Video and
Film Production workshops. Other introductory courses offer background in the
elements of film grammar and film history.
Advanced work consists primarily of inde-
pendent projects conceived by the student,
and produced either alone or with collabo-
rators. The portfolio required for admission
should include film, video or photographic
work done by the applicant and plans
for a project.

Film Graphics (Experimental Animation)
(M.F.A., B.F.A., Certificate)
This program offers students introductory
exposure to a wide range of animation
styles and techniques. Subjects covered
include design and preparation, as well as
instruction in the operation of the Oxberry
animation stand, the optical printer, and
sound recording and mixing equipment.
Subsequent work is highly individualized,
guided by the student's imagination and
personal vision. Prior experience in animation for filmmaking is not necessary or
required. The portfolio should show an
applicant's artistic interests and abilities.
Examples of animated films and other
visual material that would suggest movement and animation should be included.
Comments on proposed animated films are
welcome and helpful to the evaluation
committee.

Ed Emshwiller, Dean
Myron Emery, Optical Printing
Jules Engel, Director of Film Graphics, Animation
Jack Hannah, Director of Character Animation
Mark Jonathan Harris, Screenwriting
T. Hee, Caricature, Character Design
Bill Jackson, Operations Manager, Video
David LeBrun, Editing
Don Levy, Film Production, Film Aesthetics
Alexander Mackendrick, Directing
John F. Mahin, Video Technology,
Video Engineering
Kris Malkiewicz, Cinematography, Film Production
Robert McCrea, Character Animation
William Moore, Color and Design
Ken O'Connor, Drawing and Perspective
Elmer Plummer, Life Drawing
Terry Sanders, Documentary Film Production,
Dramatic Film Production
Michael Scroggins, Experimental Video
Chick Strand, Personal and Experimental
Live Action
Don Worthen, Sound Recording and Mixing

Facilities and Equipment
• 16mm professional sound cameras
• fully equipped sound-stages for film
  and video production
• video synthesizer and special effects
  equipment
• editing rooms with flatbed or upright
  Moviolas
• mixing theatre with eight-channel
  console
• portable and studio sound recording
  equipment
• Oxberry animation stands
• optical printer
• Bijou theatre for screenings and
  study
• Advent room

EATRE

cting Dean,
rts Design and Technology,

Jules Aaron, Evolution of the Drama,
Seminars, Directing

Robert Benedetti, Script Analysis, Acting,
Directing

Orville "Doc" Ballard, Dance Production
and Lighting

Fran Bennett, Movement

•Gill Dennis, Acting, Directing, Writing

Linda deVries, Voice Speech, Acting

Martha Ferrara, Costumier, Costume Design

•Oscar Giner, Evolution of the Drama,
Seminars, Directing

Ken Kuta, Stage Management

Lewis Palter, Acting

Frank Pendle, Technical Director, Stagecraft

Gordon Robertson, Shop Foreman,
Set Construction

Neil Schettler, Voice

Sherry Tschernisch, T'ai Chi Ch'uan

•on leave 1980–81

Fold-out posters from

the 1982 / 83

admissions bulletin

e Arts
19 82

19 79

28. 17 "Student Choir"

California Institute of the Arts

1981/82 + 1982/83

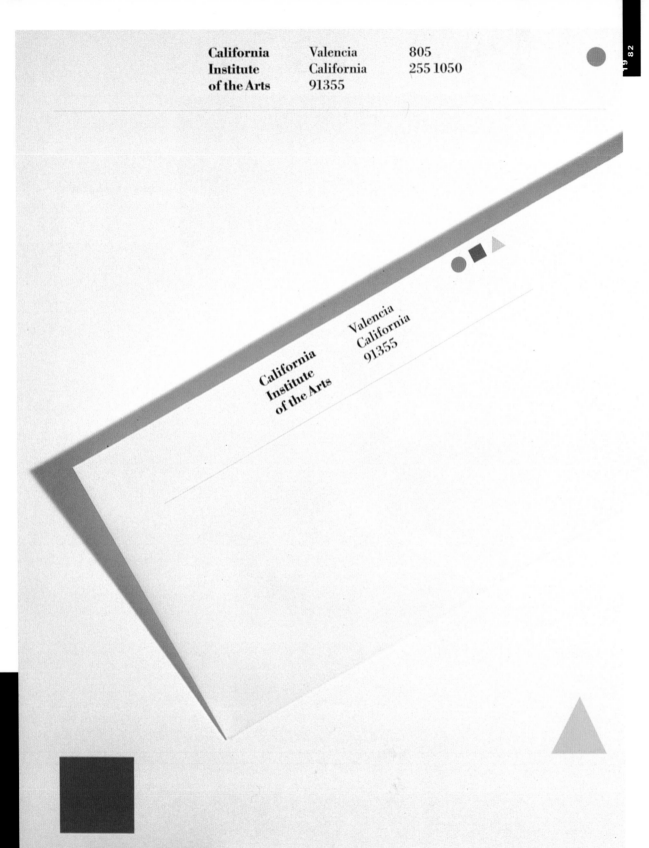

California
Institute
of the Arts
Valencia
California
91355
805
255 1050

1982

California
Institute
of the Arts
Valencia
California
91355

CalArts letterhead

unty Museum of Art

bition at the
ty Museum of Art.

The color gradations were

produced by hand

with color spray paint.

This layer was then

photographed as a single

composition, with

type added in the tradi-

tional manner in the

paste-up to complete the

poster art, which was

ultimately printed in four-

color offset.

Los Angeles County
Museum of Art

in

ART IN
LOS ANGELES

Seventeen
Artists
in the Sixties

The Museum
as Site: S i x t e e n
P r o j e c t s

21 July–
4 October
1 9 8 1

This exhibition was made possible
by a grant from the
James Irvine Foundation

1981 by Museum Associates,
Los Angeles County Museum of Art

L o s A n g e l e s C o u n t y Museum of Art
5905 Wilshire Boulevard

Art in Los Angeles

The Museum as Site: Sixteen Projects

Michael Asher
Lloyd Hamrol
Richard Jackson
John Baldessari
Jay McCafferty
Michael Brewster
Robert Graham
Chris Burden
Karen Carson
Alexis Smith
Terry Schoonhoven
Robert Irwin
Eric Orr
Michael C. McMillen
Roland Reiss
Jonathan Borofsky

Los Angeles County Museum of Art

The cut corner of the related catalog was considered graphic design heresy at the time

Collaboration with Jayme Odgers

One of the posters officially produced for the 1984 Olympics, held in Los Angeles.

This image combines an original photograph by Jayme Odgers of a swimmer, cropped and collaged against a sprayed and painted Day-Glo background that I created and silkscreened. The camera and hand working together.

Odgers added art for the cast shadow of the extended foot and leg, and the Olympics symbol and typography are generic to the series.

Los Angeles 1984 Olympic Games

1981

joan la barbara

as lightning comes, in flashes

Joan La Barbara

Album cover for a recording by Joan La Barbara, "As Lightning Comes in Flashes."

Joan La Barbara is known for using her voice as a complex musical instrument.

In traditional terms, this image expresses the idea of electricity / lightning, and, with its L.E.D. typography, anticipates the spirit, if not the technique, of the later electronic collages.

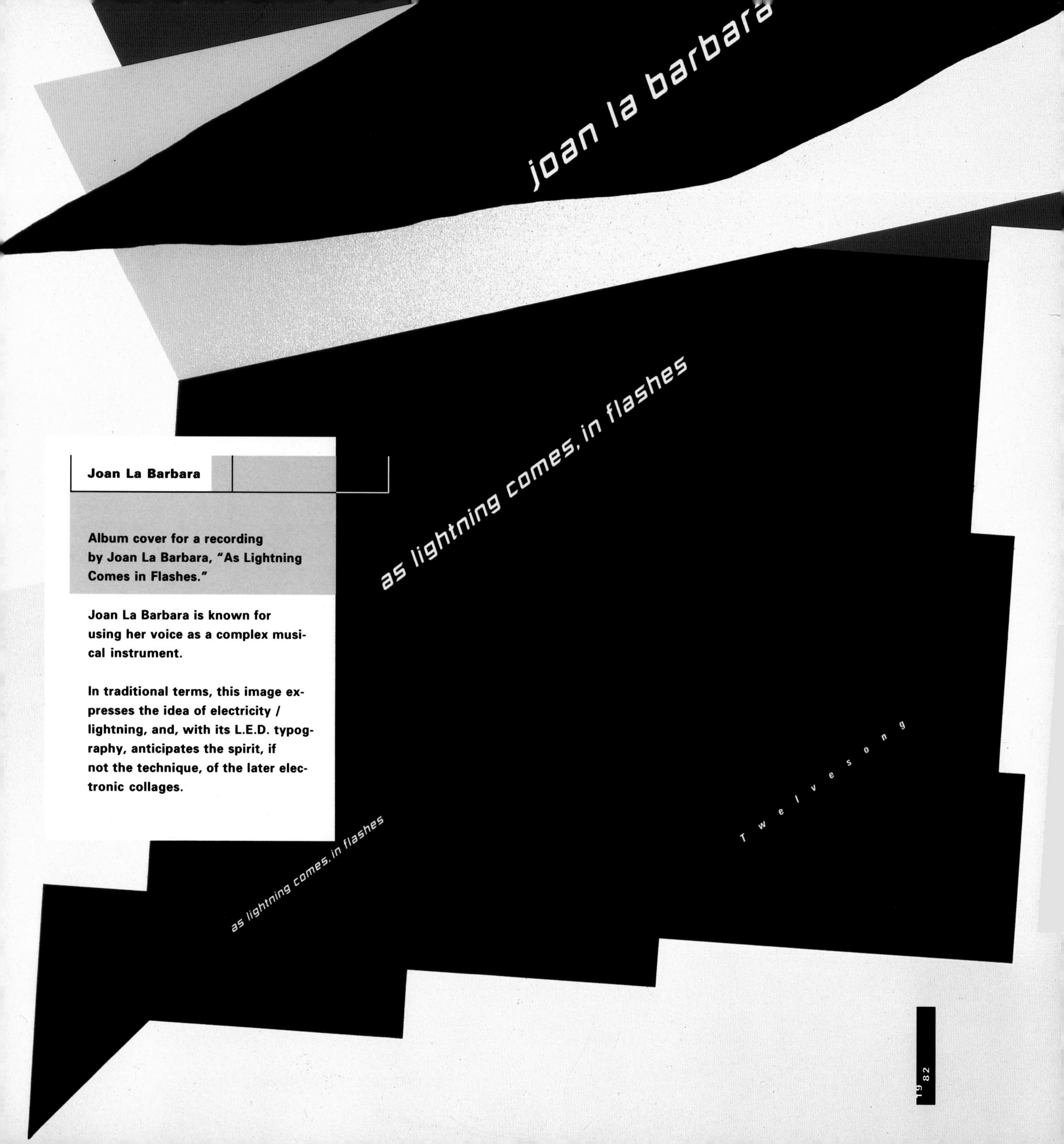

as lightning comes, in flashes

Twelvesong

19 82

A 3-D poster (and glasses) to announce the International Contract Furniture Symposium during WestWeek, an event sponsored by the PDC 2, Los Angeles.

The many disparate companies represented at Westweek (lighting, floor covering, furniture, etc.) were represented by a visual concept that unifies them all: space; in this case, outer space.

In the poster "layering" becomes a literal component of the design, in which different levels of the composition exist at different perceptual levels, in a "real" three-dimensional space. The starry universe is felt to be the rearmost environment in which all other levels exist.

Seven Graphic Designers

A poster adapted from a
double-page spread in the book
Seven Graphic Designers.

Typography, typographic rules, the
I Ching symbol Kên (keeping still),
"hashi," and three-color photographs
coexist as one personal "idea-com-
position" I created uniquely for the
book. The large photograph is an
inverted picture of a Japanese bridge
reflected in the koi pond it bridges.
"Hashi" stands for both "bridge" and
"chopsticks" (the bridge from the
hand to the mouth). Collective / individual and man / woman are some
of the dualities brought together in
the image.

H A S H I

the bridge.

Mitsumura Printing Company

water — death, ocean, rivers,
ponds, rain, snow, drowning, the
fool, moon, baths, sexual energy,
psychic energy, waves, fish, —
the abyss, snakes, magic, veils.

"In many cases there is a picture in the foreground but the sense lies far in the background"

L. Wittgenstein

"Design must seduce, shape, and perhaps more importantly, evoke emotional response."

—— AG

Video

In 1982, April Greiman became director of the program in Visual Communication at the California Institute of the Arts (CalArts). One reason for taking this position was her interest in expanding her own ideas into a curriculum; another was her interest in exposure to CalArts' electronic studios.

Though digital technology had not yet reached CalArts, state-of-the-art video equipment was there in abundance. Working primarily with a video synthesizer, originally installed at the Institute by Nam June Paik, Greiman produced a series of slides shot from a monitor of a number of manipulated video images. These "video textures" or "video landscapes," as she calls them, were the first in her personal library of electronic images. Today, this library serves as one resource for present and future hybrid compositions.

Greiman's professional work began to merge video imagery with print graphics, shifting from the illusion of a three-dimensional space on a two-dimensional surface to a more conceptual "layered" suggestion of space through overlapping imagery. The term "information / texture" came to symbolize this brief transitional period in which the open weave of the video raster (the grid of horizontal scan lines which make up a regular video image) began to redefine her conception of the hybrid image. — EM

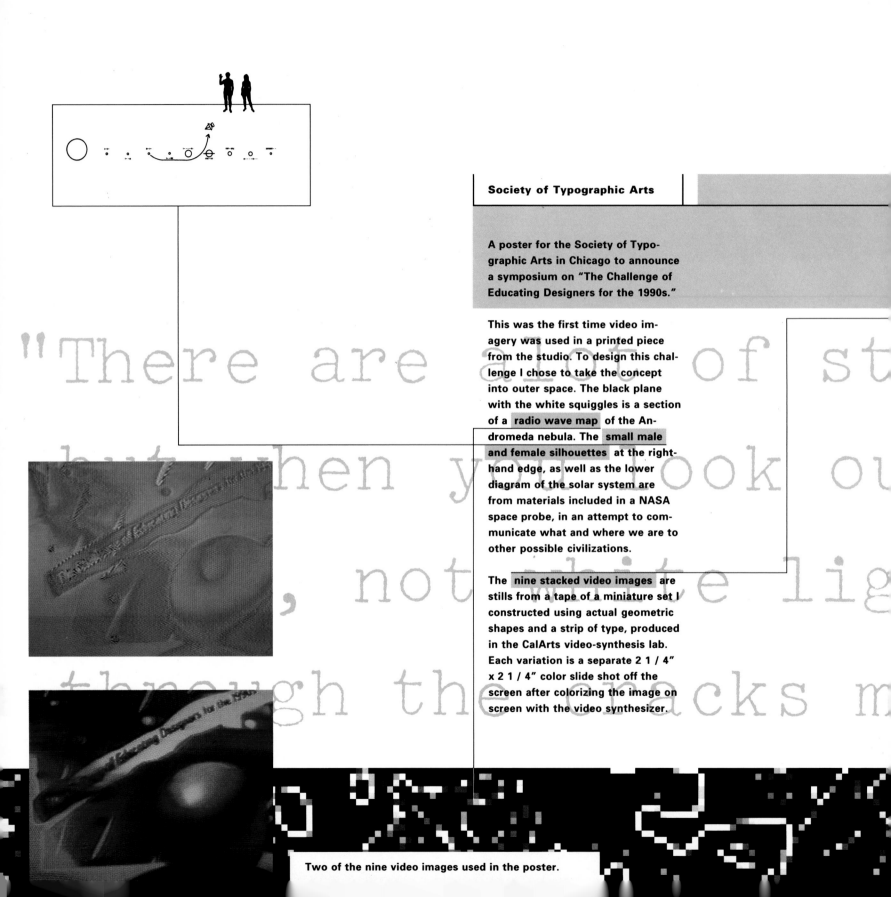

Society of Typographic Arts

A poster for the Society of Typographic Arts in Chicago to announce a symposium on "The Challenge of Educating Designers for the 1990s."

This was the first time video imagery was used in a printed piece from the studio. To design this challenge I chose to take the concept into outer space. The black plane with the white squiggles is a section of a radio wave map of the Andromeda nebula. The small male and female silhouettes at the right-hand edge, as well as the lower diagram of the solar system are from materials included in a NASA space probe, in an attempt to communicate what and where we are to other possible civilizations.

The nine stacked video images are stills from a tape of a miniature set I constructed using actual geometric shapes and a strip of type, produced in the CalArts video-synthesis lab. Each variation is a separate 2 1 / 4" x 2 1 / 4" color slide shot off the screen after colorizing the image on screen with the video synthesizer.

Two of the nine video images used in the poster.

"There are alot of stars out there
you see
out, you fall
white light. You
s more easily
hit the sun.

The Challenge of Educating Designers for the 1990's

September 23, 24, 25 1983
Illinois Institute of Technology

STA + Women in Design

re easily

The completed poster

19 82

47

Ron Rezek

A silk-screen promotional poster for Ron Rezek, a designer and manufacturer of lighting fixtures.

This image seems simple at first glance, but a closer look shows its complexity:

- The central luminous glow coming out of the overall yellow-to-white printer's gradation is an airbrushed oval.

- The standing lamps on the outer edges are coarse halftone color separations from color slide originals.

- The top and bottom images (lamp and classical head; foot and lamp pedestal) are also separations from color slides. These slides were taken of freeze-frames from playback of a videotape shot in the studio. Tissue outlines on the final paste-up indicate the particular silhouette, or cutout, each video image was to conform to.

- Finally, all color separations (separate runs of color in silk screening) were deliberately misaligned and further tinkered with after viewing the initial proofs; sometimes holding back part of a black screen, sometimes shifting one run of color out of register with another.

RON REZEK
LIGHTING+
FURNITURE

The completed poster

Simpson Paper Company

A poster produced for the Simpson Paper Company's annual promotional poster series.

The dominant imagery here is sections of individual video textures, originally generated and shot as color transparencies at my studio. The grid lines and dots, the white paint stipple, and the signature were produced by hand.

The bottom title strip is generic to the "Sequences" series. The small "in / form / ation / texture" phrase was set conventionally and added to the paste-up. The large, blocky, vertically aligned letters spelling out "information texture" were created on the Macintosh computer, together with their inner textures. The word "texture" encloses a printer's gradation from orange to white.

information / texture

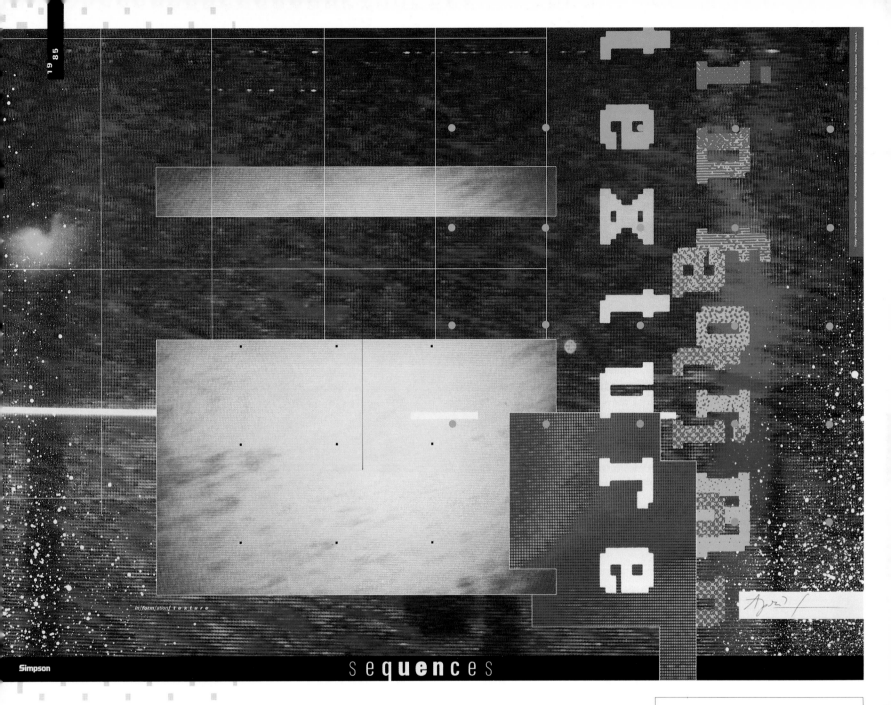

The completed poster

Video Fabric

This "video landscape" for the Polyester Institute of Japan is a translation of a video image into a four-color print on synthetic fabric.

First, I selected freeze-frames from existing studio tapes of manipulated video imagery. These freeze-frames were photographed from the screen as 4" x 5" color transparencies, which the printer then translated into conventional four-color separations. What is unconventional is that the image was ultimately printed on fabric and not paper.

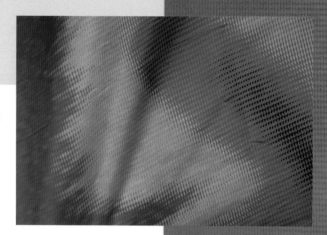

Esprit Television Spots

A series of twelve ten-second commercials for Esprit: six for "Esprit Kids" and six for "Esprit Sport."

This project was my first production exclusively in video. The approach I used was to animate pre-existing color transparencies of models in a variety of active poses. The slides were first transferred to video and then manipulated with ADO postproduction video capabilities, creating rapid "slide-show" sequences from the slides, then adding visual transitions (zooms and wipes), and text.

I also composed the synchronized sound tracks on a sound synthesizer, using live voices which were tightly edited in the same spirit as the visuals.

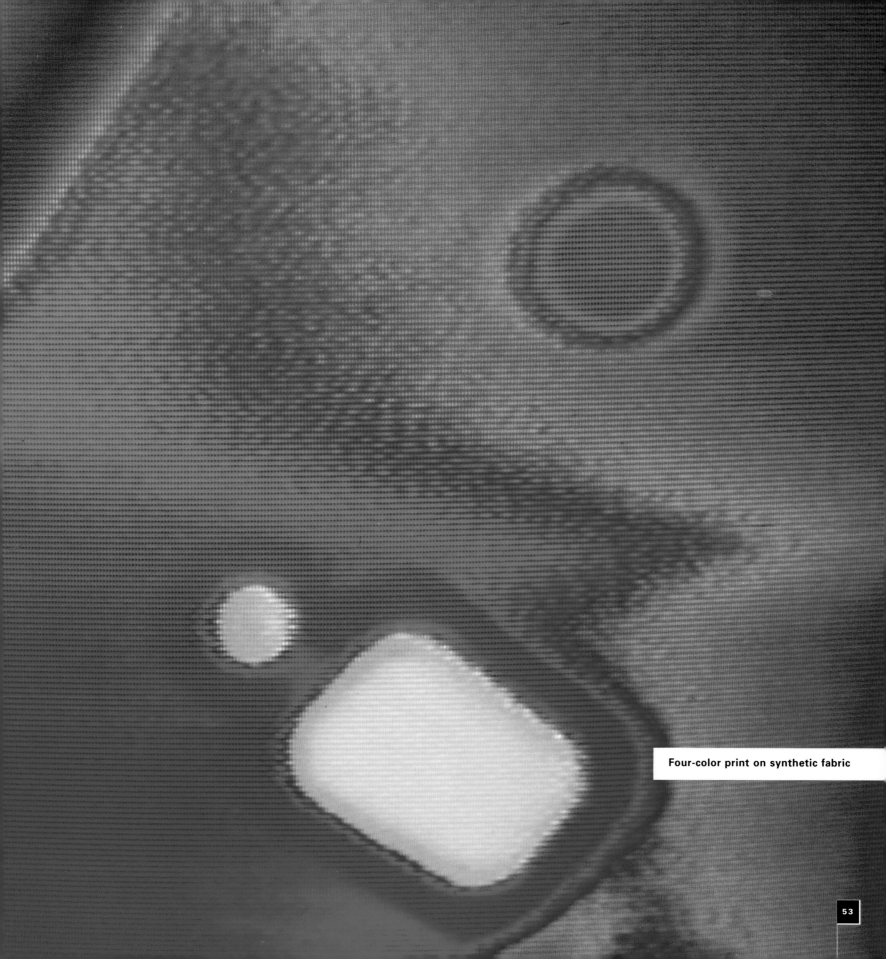

Four-color print on synthetic fabric

"The computer is just another pencil" — AG

Macintosh

Since its introduction in 1984, the Macintosh computer has rapidly become an essential tool for designers, not only for familiar tasks but also for its ability to suggest entirely new solutions.

At April Greiman Inc it was immediately recognized for what it is—a new paradigm, a conceptual "magic slate" opening up a new era of opportunity for graphic artists. It has since become an integral part of every project at many levels: brainstorming, camera-ready art, typesetting, electronic page composition, and on and on in ever-expanding applications. A single Macintosh in the studio has grown to several, including a number of peripheral devices, among them a FAX machine and modem to converse with sophisticated printers, and clients and co-workers at remote sites. Everyone in the studio is fluent with the Macintosh as well as with the traditional tools, using them interdependently.

The renowned friendly Macintosh environment, with its cozy iconic mimicry of familiar tools like erasers and paintbrushes, makes it supremely easy to use. At the same time, this reassuring familiarity obscures what is provocative about this new tool, much of which contradicts ordinary practice:

• The "Undo" function allows you to take back something you just did, without a trace; or, with another click, restores it. The traditional way of thinking would call this a great way to correct mistakes. In fact, you learn to think of it as a means to attempt them. Mistakes are accidents, and accidents often reveal unexpected possibilities.

• It's so easy to edit as you go along that editing becomes part of the original act of creation, instead of being something "done later." This is wonderful, but takes getting used to.

• It makes so many things that were so hard so easy that there's a renewed emphasis on why you're doing what you're doing in the first place. In other words, how good is your original idea?

"What we are discovering is a new texture, a new design language, a new landscape in communications. As people become empowered with this tool we'll see terrible things and wonderful things. We will learn from it as designers. Everybody is visual, it's in the collective soul. I like the idea that so many people will have a common language using modems and electronic bulletin boards. It's spreading like crazy."

— AG

55

"Or an accident will happen and you'll say, 'Oh, that's terrific, let's go that way!' Then you're off on a whole new idea. This pioneering, where you don't have an aesthetic and you don't have a tradition, is both time-consuming and wonderful. To feel lost is great; there are only a few areas in this very controlled industry where you can feel that."— AG

• Nothing is ever "finished" in the conventional sense. The paint never dries in the Mac úniverse. You may stop working on a piece any time you wish, but you may also, years later, wake up a document and go right on manipulating it as if you had never stopped. Everything is always alive.

• Similarly, the "immortality" of the objects you create, together with the ease of editing, encourages the development of a personal library of imagery which may have many un-expected uses over time.

• There is no "original" in the usual sense. Every copy is identical to the original, unlike traditional forms of reproduction. And this "copy" is also, by definition, in the exact form to be electronically communicated to others.

• At the same time, the issue of "what's whose?" rears its head. When it's so easy to scan (the digi-tal version of making a Xerox copy) from existing sources (books, maga-zines, photographs, etc.) and seam-lessly incorporate the product into your image, who owns what? The collaging and reprocessing tendency built into this environment blurs traditional boundaries in sometimes confusing ways.

• You are always working in a state of visual perfection. The first word of your first vague thought is in high-resolution 12 pt. Univers 55 type, or whatever. Even raw begin-nings have a finished look.

• Perhaps the most profound implica-tion for the future is that digital technology collapses all media into a single desktop tool speaking one digital language. It is really a single **metamedium**. A sound is gener-ated, edited, and remembered as a unique pattern of the same com-puter "bits" (on / off electronic impulses) that describe a color, for example. This is why the generic Mac "Cut and Paste" function is so effortless. Previously separate me-dia begin to diffuse, to merge with others. Cut a picture, paste it into a song. A **word** is a **color** is a **sound** is a **movement**. The new significant media are **hybrids**. The age of the specialist is replaced by the age of the **dedicated generalist**. — EM

"What I experience is rather than doing something more quickly, we're looking at more possibilities. Instead of doing less work we are seeing more options. Ordinarily, you wouldn't try twelve different sizes of headline type because it would involve setting it and statting it for each variation. It's too expensive and takes too much time. But with the Mac, once the information is stored you can look at 72,000 variations immediately."

AG

Macintosh Fabric

A "Mac landscape" is translated onto synthetic fabric for the Polyester Institute of Japan.

Original Macintosh texture

Synthetic fabric

A poster collage for
Design Quarterly magazine.

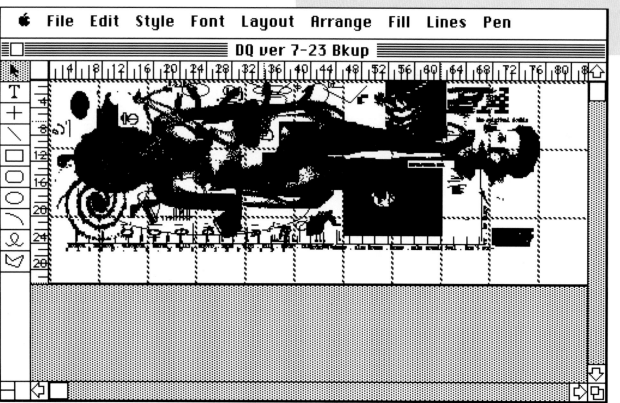

É   File   Edit   Style   Font   Layout   Arrange   Fill   Lines   Pen

DQ ver 7-23 Bkup

Design Quarterly is a publication
of the Walker Art Center in Minnea-
polis, directed to the international
design community. Each issue
takes on a single topic, or occasionally represents the work of a single
designer. Mickey Friedman, the
remarkable editor of this extraordinary publication, offered me
an issue of my own to see what
I would do.

My idea for the issue was to do it as
a 2' x 6' poster that folds down
to fit in a sleeve the size of a regular
copy of the magazine. The poster
was to be a personal experiment in
which one side was a life-size
collage created entirely on the
Macintosh, and the other side car-
ried a variety of related text and
video images.

The actual screen image
of the entire 2' x 6'
collage, in its "Reduce to
Fit" size on screen.
A number of views are
possible, from "Actual
Size" (close-up) to succes-

sively smaller but more
inclusive views. Each view
gives you access to
the MacDraw tool set the
same as any other.

Although the collage was made of
many different text and graphic
elements, it was created and printed
out entirely on the Macintosh as one
document. In other words, no
conventional paste-up; it was all
composed on screen and printed
out as is, on 8 1/2" x 11" sheets of
bond paper.

(text continues on page 67)

this document is 284k

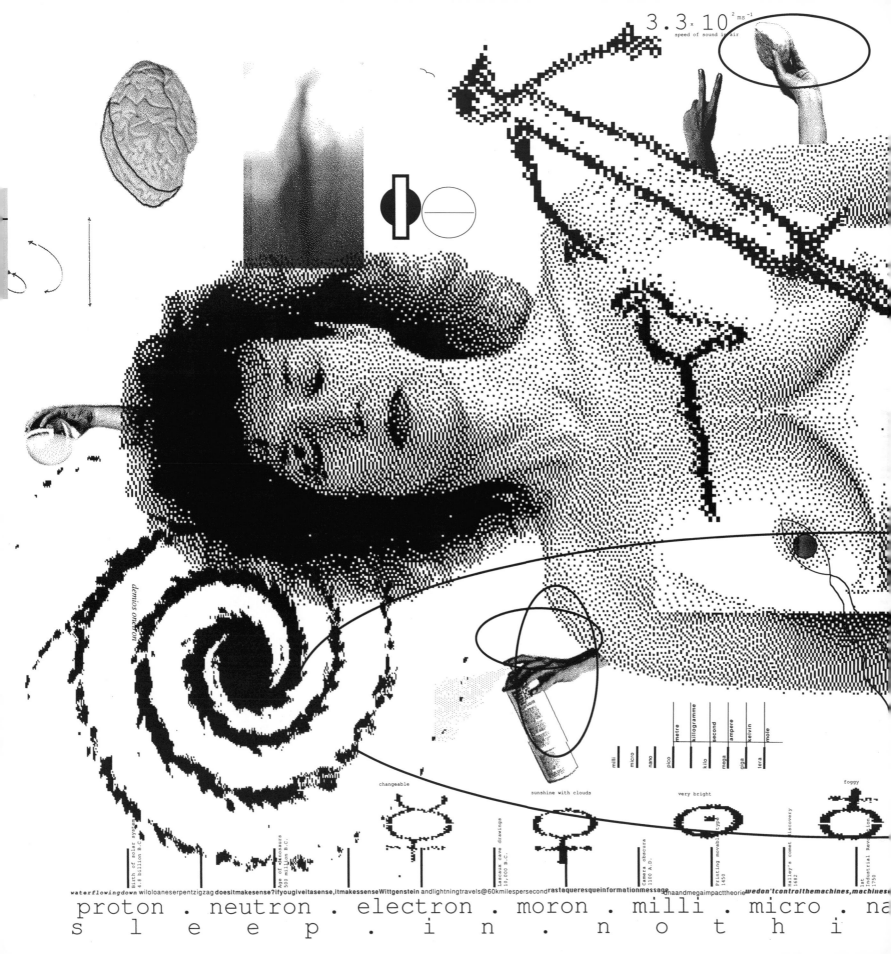

$3.3 \times 10^{2}\ ms^{-1}$
speed of sound in air

demios oneiron

waterflowingdown wiloloaneserpentzigzag doesitmakesense?ifyougiveitasense,itmakessenseWittgenstein andlightningtravels@60kmilespersecond rastaqueresqueinformationmessage naandmegaimpacttheorie wedon'tcontrolthemachines,machines

changeable

sunshine with clouds

very bright

foggy

Birth of solar system
4.8 billion B.C.

Age of dinosaurs
500 million B.C.

Lascaux cave drawings
10,000 B.C.

Camera obscura
1100 A.D.

Printing movable type
1450

Halley's comet discovery
1682

1st Industrial Revolution
1750

milli   micro   nano   pico   metre   kilogramme   second   ampere   kelvin   mole   kilo   mega   giga   tera

proton . neutron . electron . moron . milli . micro . na

s l e e p . i n . n o t h i

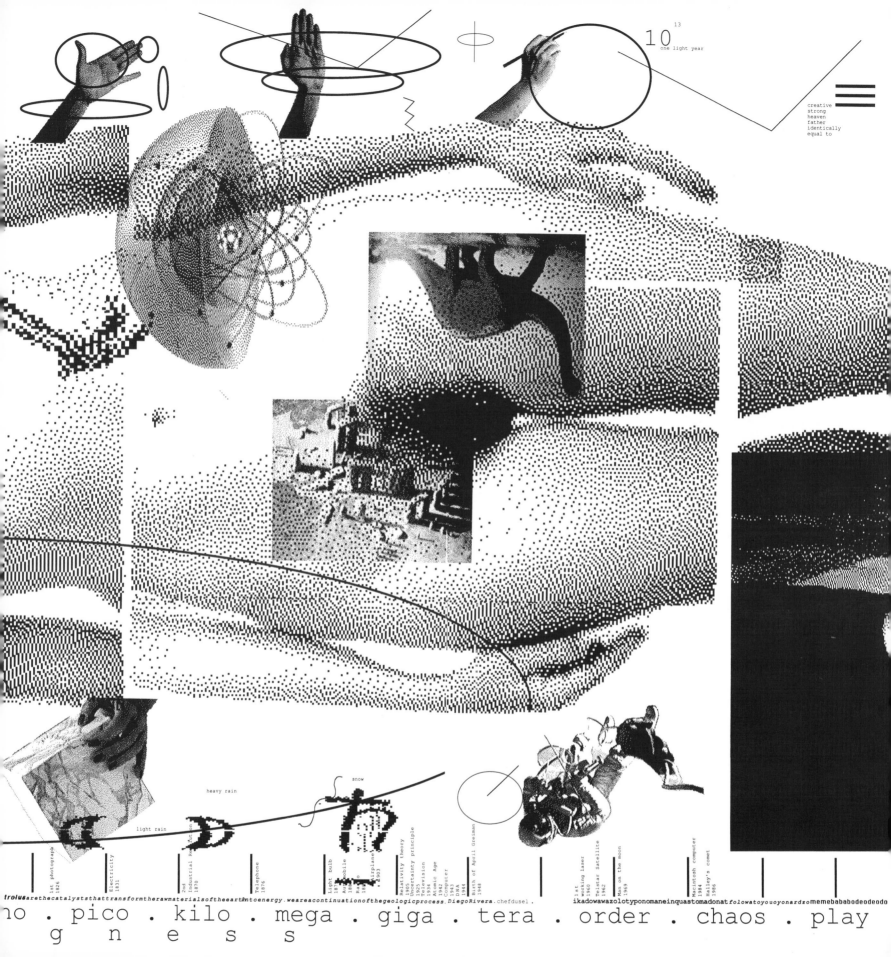

creative
strong
heaven
father
identically
equal to

10^{13}
one light year

snow

heavy rain

light rain

| | | | | | | | | | | | | | | | | | | | |

1st photograph 1826
Electricity 1831
2nd Industrial Revolution 1870
Telephone 1876
Light bulb 1879
Automobile 1884
Radio 1896
Airplane 1903
Relativity theory 1905
Uncertainty principle 1925
Television 1934
Atomic Age 1942
Computer 1943
DNA 1944
Birth of April Greiman 1948
1st working laser 1960
Telstar Satellite 1962
Man on the moon 1969
Macintosh computer 1984
Halley's comet 1986

trolus arethecatalyststhattransformtherawmaterialsoftheearthintoenergy.weareacontinuationofthegeologicprocess.*DiegoRivera*.chefdusel.   ikadowawazolotyponomaneinquastomadonat*folowatoyouoyonardro*memebababodeodeodo

no . pico . kilo . mega . giga . tera . order . chaos . play

g   n   e   s   s

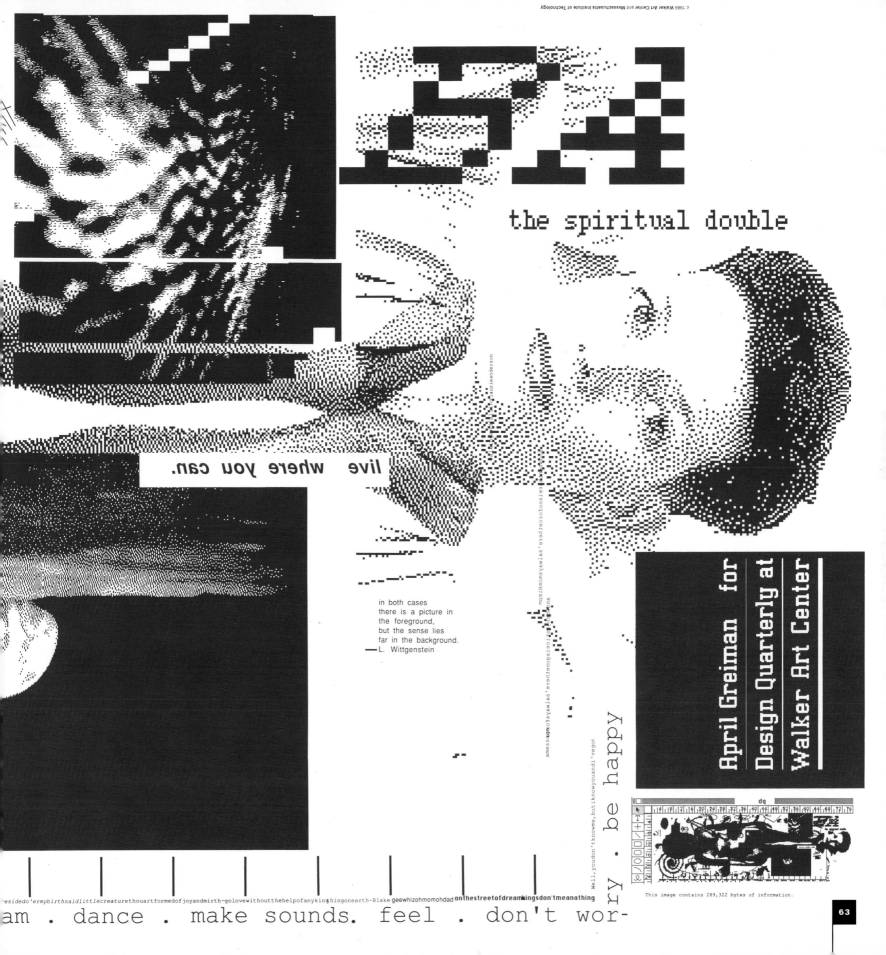

So I'm walking through the English Garden with Andreas--and I mention the idea (duality) of order and chaos. So, he tips me off to the latest philosophical twist--chaos is simply a man/mind-made invention that frankly doesn't exist! I think about this and I say...yea, come to think about it, in seeing a computer model of fractal geometry, things that appear without structure, such as clouds and mountains, are in fact orderly processes. While on the surface, things seem irregular and chaotic, when you break down the parts, in reality they are more and more modular and ordered. The more finitely we perceive them, the more their inherent order becomes apparent.

So, I was lying in bed. I felt like I was in a small boat. The waves started to well up. A slight feeling of nausea came over me. The swells got bigger. I was rocking up and down, side to side. I couldn't stop the wave. It got rougher and rougher. I slammed from side to side. I used every bit of consciousness to remain in balance/ not to fall off. With my right palm on the solar plexus I was able to ride it out until it quieted down several hours later.

We were
noon.
incredib
started
what we
sway fr
in the r
was pul
pressure
swayed
we were
and onte
others
journey

The Zen monk starts on his daily walk through the forest. A young student follows behind, hoping to discover some secrets of his master along the way. Deep in the forest the master comes across a giant boulder fallen across the path, making it impossible to continue forward on the journey. The monk meditates for a few short moments and then goes into the forest and gets a large tree branch, which he then uses as a lever to gently roll the rock out of his path. The master continues on but the young student, terribly excited to have witnessed this, grabs the stick and runs back to the monastery to impress the others with the discovery: when you encounter an obstacle find a stick.

The moral of the story is that it isn't about the stick, it's about how to continue the journey.

...this story reminds me of my particular journey with this piece. In the beginning the obstacle was simply to master the Macintosh technology and software used to generate text and image. The image was ultimately composed in MacDraw, a program which permits large scale (up to 4 x 8 foot) collaging of digitized and drawn images electronically cut and pasted from MacPaint. The collage is just out of the LaserWriter as separate 8 1/2 x 11 inch sheets which are then assembled together.

This issue of DQ began over one year ago when Robert Jensen, Graphic Designer for the Walker, invited me to do an issue on my work. I can't remember being so flattered and, simultaneously, so scared by an invitation. Without knowing what format it would take I knew it would involve something of all the technology I had been throwing myself at over the past three years. Soon after, Robert left the Walker and I began my discussions with Mickey Friedman, an inspired, sympathetic client. I never enjoyed anything so much, or laughed so hard while developing a project.

About the time I had the thought to use MacDraw software on the Mac to layer and compose all the bits I had been collecting, I contacted Marv Zweier (from the printer, George Rice and Sons). I wanted to know the possibilities for printing an oversized image. He told me that he could find a plant to print the piece (Ivy Hill) but that the maximum size that I could design for was 2 x 6 feet. It was then that I decided to create an actual-size image of myself as the underlying idea. (Marv, huge tears well up when I think of how you bail me out all the time; I absolutely could not have done this work without you.)

The genius of MacDraw is that you can input an image/idea /object and then literally stretch it on screen from a few inches to a few feet in a matter of seconds. You can compose the entire 4 x 8 foot image right in front of you — altering, adding, layering, trying different compositions-changing meaning and form with a click of the mouse. It's a miracle! You can move things around freely on the surface working at large scale or diving into actual size any time you see fit - in and out, small to large, dense to sparse, complicated to simple. Text was added in MacDraw and manipulated in the same manner.

For six months I gathered materials; for three months I sketched (MacPaint) and digitized images (MacVision). For another three months I composed, layered, and stretched (MacDraw) and finally produced this piece on my LaserWriter. In the middle of the process it seemed we were perfectly matched —my ideas and the ease and speed of the software. It enabled an extraordinary fluidity in a complex creative process. It made possible placing and altering new imagery or text in the space until it became unable to handle all the layering of information I came to want. Ultimately, the speed with which I threw it into overload. System Errors kept popping up, making it impossible to print out the final image. One night I left the printer on to print overnight, since it takes a fair amount of time for it to process this much information. In the morning when I returned to the studio I saw that the printout had left out the entire bottom half of my body. When I looked at the screen to see what was going on, I noticed that my entire body was no longer there! Everything else layered on top of my former self was as plain as day. So, somewhere, near the planet Pluto, we believe, a 5 foot 4 1/2 inch digitized image of April Greiman is orbiting.

My absolute genius assistant, Ron Romero, finally tricked the software into printing out, helping me to create the original digitized images, and providing me with constant support in the studio, including back-rubs when I had contorted myself into silly-putty.

Then we thought about a staple to bind it to the cover. I was afraid that it would tear no matter how gently it would be pulled. The appearance of the piece would be ruined. I thought it would be good if it didn't bind in at all. We're thinking about putting it in the Walker's envelope—but what about when it needs to be on a shelf? And what about the necessary printed spine? So my last thought is a slipcase with a printed spine. First it was to be glued, but the budget didn't allow that ....then I resolved it with a slotted tab and a diagonal cut. This was all fine—the new size of the piece was slightly under 9 x 12 inches, with a slipcase of 9 x 12 inches. Then we talked to Mickey...who said that the envelopes were 9 x 12 inches! So that was that!

Back to the drawing board. We looked finally at the 2 x 6 foot piece and how it folded. The 11 inch dimension that folded twice left an awkward 2 inch strip and the 8 1/2 inch dimension folded eight times left an equally odd strip of 4 inches. So, I naturally let the piece grow to 33 x 76 1/2 inches. We checked with the paper company to see if their custom sheet size could accommodate this-- it was a go, and. so the piece evolved and grew. What that meant in terms of MacDraw is that I continued to layer and layer more information. The thought of making it any smaller had practically left my mind completely. Then the bindery said they wouldn't fold this for less than 75 cents apiece if it went wider than 22 inches since it would be hand-folded! Typical obstacle. The printer then jumped in and offered (for slightly more money, of course) to put a scoring plate on the press so that the hand-folding could simply accordion and then have two hand-folds. Our problems seemed over, once again. Then the printer mentioned that they had planned to print two-up and so 33 inches was an impossibility without doubling the press time and cost. These technical production problems were being handled by the production master of my life, Karlee Greene. At no time did she ever stop pushing to help me get it exactly the way I saw it. She would ask any supplier anything, anytime. This woman is an absolute whiz at most everything that has to do with the creative process.

So, with some juggling on the Mac and moving text to the back side of the poster, we were finally able to get it down to 25 1/2 x 76 1/2 inches. Meanwhile, System Errors were occurring—stretched images were printing with white scan lines due to incompatible software between the Mac and the LaserWriter—entire days are devoted to trying to figure out how to print the monster. We also learned the hard lesson about making backup copies...a cardinal lesson in all of this. Or really the lesson of NOT making backup copies of disks, is more like it!

Finally, I would like to thank Eric Martin - the real inspiration for all of this. Without his encouragement, instruction, patience and love this would not have become a reality.

We're riding in a small plane together/ I am the pilot/ we are both wearing headsets/ Eric's headset is plugged into my left ear. Thank you Eric.

p.s. Harry Marks introduced me to the Mac, believe it or not, in Macy's in Carmel! He has been my early tech-guru wapapal. And so I remain, indebted forever. And to Kurt Sickert, whose photograph of me appears on the back of the slipcase and who opened a door for me that has taught me to look at it from the other side. To Andreas Kemmerling's love from the background. To Paul Hinckley – always -there -with- the- big-important -stuff. Thanks to JG, Edith, Muriel, Kath and Rhonda for all their selfless support throughout the process.

Thank You
George Rice and Sons
Coordination, separations, stripping and printing on slipcase
Ivy Hill
Printing of the poster
Area Trade
Binding
Macintosh / LaserWriter
Typesetting

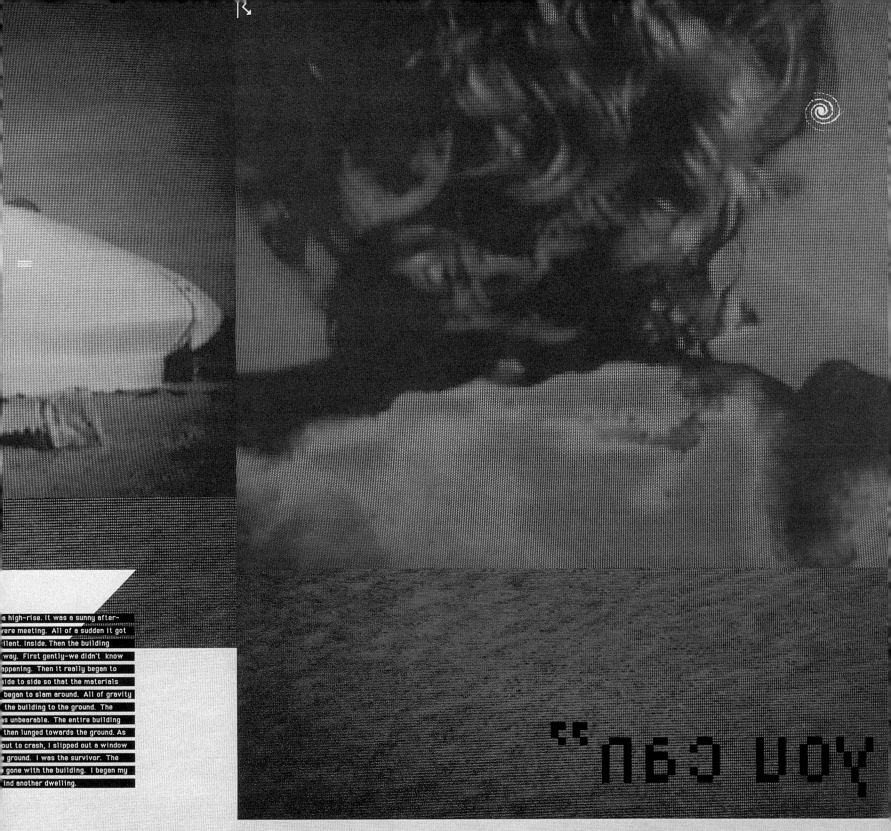

"Π68Ͻ ⴑOꓯ

a high-rise. It was a sunny after-
were meeting. All of a sudden it got
ilent. Inside. Then the building
way. First gently-we didn't know
appening. Then it really began to
side to side so that the materials
began to slam around. All of gravity
the building to the ground. The
s unbearable. The entire building
then lunged towards the ground. As
out to crash, I slipped out a window
ground. I was the survivor. The
gone with the building. I began my
ind another dwelling.

The signature line, "made in space by April Greiman," tells us a number of things about this unique artist/designer: she possesses an original wit; she means to expand the traditional two dimensional surface of graphic design into the multiple layers of the third dimension; and, she accomplishes this by applying a creative mix of old and new technologies to graphic problems.

In this issue of Design Quarterly, Greiman has used the computer to create a large-format montage that defies the magazine norm. The usual thirty-two pages of DQ are reorganized into a single-page poster filled with ideograms and thoughts about the creation of man--a large-format topic! Visual poetics, impossible to achieve without the magical transformations of the thinking machines (in this case Apple's Macintosh programs MacDraw, MacPaint and MacVision on one side and video and Macintosh texture-imagery on the reverse), are the result.

April Greiman's work with electronic media comes out of her earlier explorations into deep space through photography. Now, stretched out moving forms create a proscenium for photographs of objects that behave like orbiting planets around a core of ideas. These experiments combine electronic impulses with photo-graphic and typographic tradition that hark back to the refinement and clarity of her Basle days.

Less talented hands have delivered a flood of computer graphics that break no design barriers. For the most part such efforts have yielded rather rigid, repetitive, formulaic results -- little content and less probing of the medium's potential.The difference in Greiman's work is her abil-ity to take the same equipment into areas of her own invention. She not only stretch-es the imagery, but she expands the ideas, developing a fresh, rich pluralism, a mix-ture of words and images that challenge previous conceptions of the limits of graphic vision.

April Greiman currently works out of a large, light-filled studio near central Los Angeles. She studied at the Kansas City Art Institute and the Allgemeine Kunstgewerbeschule in Basle, under the tutelage of Armin Hofmann and Wolfgang Weingart. After several years of teaching, she was named Program Director of Visual Communications at the California Institute of the Arts in 1982, where she served through 1984. For a new client, she has recently created a series of colorful ten-second video spots--the promising start of a daring new adventure in space.

Mildred Friedman

(text continued from page 60)

The software used to bring all the elements together was MacDraw, ordinarily thought of as a basic drafting program. The genius of MacDraw is that you can input a tremendous variety of images and then layer, size, and push them around in a matter of seconds. A few other things made MacDraw right for this project:

• It accepts digitized images from the MacVision digitizer, which takes the image from a video camera and translates it into a quasi-photographic dot (pixel) image on the Mac screen that may then be edited with MacPaint tools. This meant that live video images of myself together with images from several sources could be brought into the MacDraw composition, where they could then be freely composed.

• Its "Text" function printed out at near typeset quality, so type didn't have to be set separately. This permitted the composition of text directly with image from the start.

• Its "Tiling" function made it possible to print out the full 2' x 6' document as a set of 8 1/2" x 11" pages, like a mosaic, which was hand assembled into the finished art by the printer.

The image is a composite of techniques. For example, the small hands which extend from the left arm aren't conventional photographs, they're digitized images. They have the same dot pattern as the body, but they've been reduced in MacDraw so the pixel texture isn't as obvious. The ovals and lines were created with the drawing tools in MacDraw.

With MacDraw, any element can be clicked on and awakened for further manipulation at any time. For instance, you can click on a block of text to tell the computer you want to change it, then edit its style, size, or orientation—even flip it so it reads backwards—and see it all, immediately, on screen.

This may all sound straightforward, but in practice it was a hair-raising adventure. MacDraw is like an intelligent, friendly, flexible assistant—until you ask it to do one too many things. Then, without warning, it can become wildly irrational, losing whole sections of an image or creating mysterious artifacts on screen.

This document became so big toward the end that it took hours to print. One morning (having let the printer work all night to produce the mosaic of pages for the latest version) it was discovered that the bottom half of my body was mysteriously missing from the printout. It also wasn't anywhere on screen. Fortunately, a back-up copy of the disk made it possible to put me back together again.

"Live whe

Los Angeles Institute of Contemporary Art

This poster for the Los Angeles Institute of Contemporary Art was the first design in which output from the Macintosh appeared in the final product from the studio.

The text for the event and date as well as the textures were created on the Macintosh, statted up, and pasted into the composition. I like the "jaggy," rough quality of the larger sizes of bit-mapped fonts (at the relatively coarse screen resolution), and continue to use them occasionally for textural contrast with high-resolution printout which is now available in the studio. The smaller type was set conventionally, as was the vertical "LAICA" (their logo) on the left edge, and the huge letters that also form the word "LAICA," of which the most apparent is the blue "A" in a Macintosh texture. In more recent pieces, with high-resolution Mac text output now available, smaller body type is often generated in the studio on the computer as well.

It may be more than coincidence that the retirement of Vernon Simpson, my longtime typesetter of choice for beautiful handset headline or body type, occurred in the same year I acquired my first Macintosh.

Macintosh textures

Fashion Show + Clothing Sale

Fashion Show
Friday Evening
February 7th
7 - 9 pm
11111
Santa Monica Blvd
22nd Floor
Donation:
$50.00 per person

Clothing Sale
Saturday & Sunday
February 8th & 9th
10 am - 6 pm
1739 Pontius
Ground Floor Warehouse
Admission Free

Sponsors and Supporters

Southern California Graphics
Cointreau Cocktails
April Greiman
L.A. Style Magazine
Esprit
Fred Segal
Michael Morrison
JAG
Jimmy'Z
Michelle Lamy
Christine Albers
Kiahn
Pamela Dewey
Theodore's
Dennis Goldsmith
Irene Sue
Camp Beverly Hills
Leon Max
Gregory Poe
Holly's Harp
Azar Woods

**Cocktail reception
hosted by
Cointreau America, Inc.**

**Choreography by
Peggy Orr**

**Food and Drink
Courtesy of
West Beach Cafe
and 72 Market Street
Julie Stone**

The completed poster

The digitized portrait

A poster announcing a talk at the Maryland Institute College of Art. All components were generated on the Mac, and assembled using conventional paste-up.

The image of my face was produced spontaneously at a party. It was the first time I played with a video "digitizer," an inexpensive software that translates a home video camera image into a fine pattern of black or white dots (pixels) on the Macintosh screen. This same technique was used later, more consciously, in the *Design Quarterly* collage, and in several other projects.

The white scribble all across my face I did as a joke at the same time. Once the image is on screen, any paint tool (brush, pencil, eraser, etc.) may be picked up and used to modify it. By some accident the image happened to be saved that evening, and many months later was remembered and recalled for this purpose.

The orange swirl is the same digitized "galaxy" image as in the *Design Quarterly* collage. This brings up an interesting point. Since it's so easy in the electronic environment to recontext and rework saved images, there is a tendency to develop a personal library of images which may find more than one use.

The yellow background is a digitized photo of sand dunes. The blue bars came from a blowup of a single Macintosh gradation which was cut, spaced apart, and pasted down. And, of course, the type was all produced on the Macintosh.

Snow White + the Seven Pixels

1986

An evening with April Greiman
presented as part of the Art Litho

Designer-in-Residence Program

Visual Presentation
8:00 pm
Thursday, November 6
1 9 8 6
Maryland Institute,
College of Art

Mount Royal Station Auditorium
Mount Royal Avenue + Cathedral Street

Reception following the lecture
in the Decker Gallery

Seating is unreserved

The completed poster

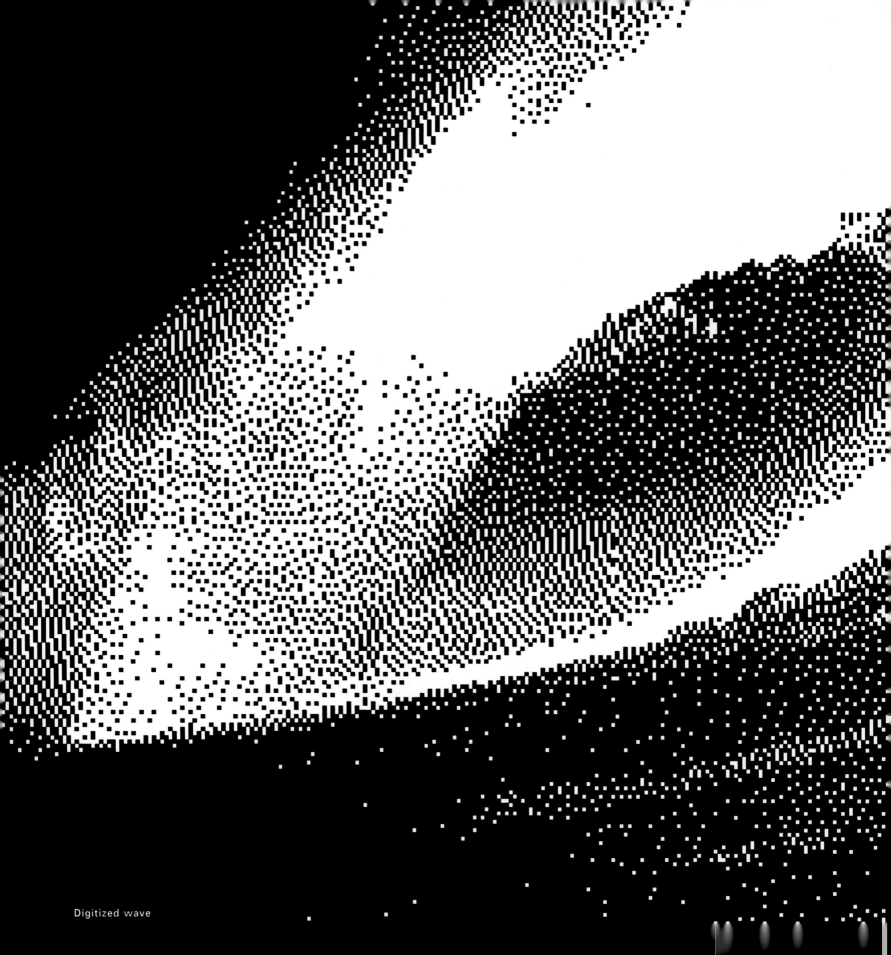
Digitized wave

Pacific Wave

A sculpture and poster

for "Pacific Wave—

California Graphic Design,"

an exhibition held

at the Fortuny

Museum in Venice, Italy.

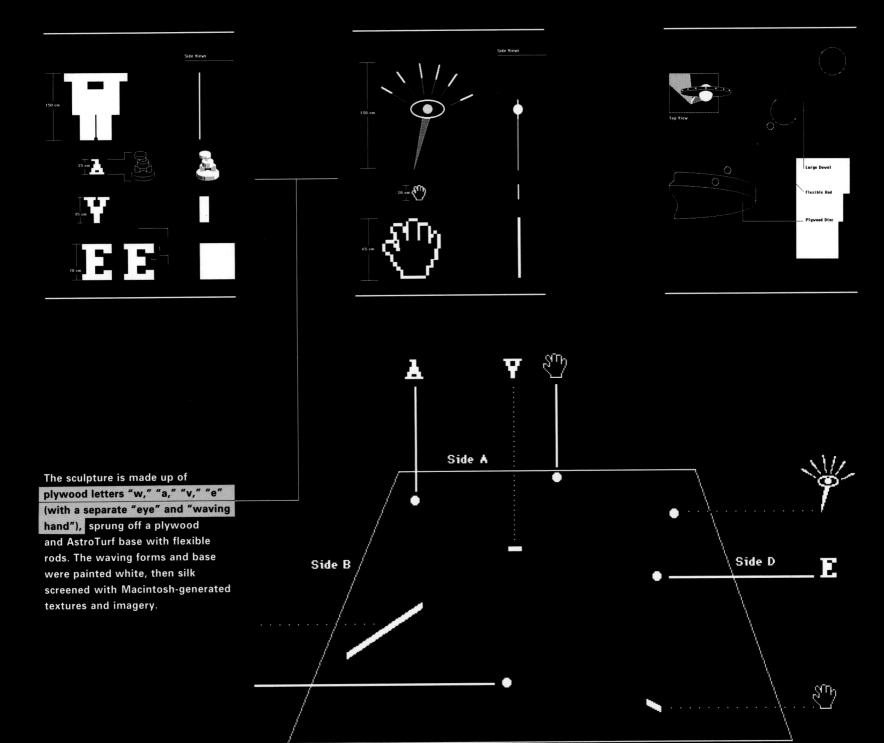

Side Views

Side Views

Top View

150 cm

25 cm

35 cm

70 cm

130 cm

20 cm

65 cm

Large Dowel

Flexible Rod

Plywood Disc

The sculpture is made up of **plywood letters "w," "a," "v," "e" (with a separate "eye" and "waving hand"),** sprung off a plywood and AstroTurf base with flexible rods. The waving forms and base were painted white, then silk screened with Macintosh-generated textures and imagery.

A

V

Side A

Side B

Side D

E

Side C

Macintosh construction documents

object suspended from springs, flexible enough to move with air currents
base of object rests on top of platform

The art for the specifications and a set of digitized images of a small foamcore model of the sculpture were created and printed out on a Macintosh in Los Angeles, then FAXed to Venice, where workmen constructed the sculpture with only this information. The model served as the means to compose the piece; the Macintosh as the translator to the workmen. To my surprise, when I arrived weeks later the result conformed exactly to my expectation!

The foamcore model, four views

The sculpture side panels,

silk screened with blown-

up Macintosh textures

The completed sculpture in Venice, Italy

The poster for the exhibition was largely Macintosh-generated. A simple paint program (FullPaint) was used to create the title type. It was then twisted into a watery profile with the "Distort" tool in the same software. The more formal tiny type (in vertical pink and black bars) was also set on the Mac. The wave image was digitized from a photograph in a surfer magazine.

The small domino-like object sitting on the wave image is a blown-up section of the coarse dot pattern (pixels) making up that image. In turn, this section was blown up again to form the giant, overall "swiss-cheese" pink and black element containing the title type. Thus there are three levels of the same image in the composition.

A non-Macintosh element is the continuous gradation in the rear layer, which was originally generated at another time on a sophisticated graphic workstation (see Chapter 4). This gradation, repeated and rotated, also defines the ink for the digitized wave. The Day-Glo pink "brush stroke" was produced by hand and then statted to its present size and included in the paste-up.

The completed poster

Stilnovo

An identity and stationery design for an importer and retailer of predominantly Italian furniture and accessories.

All art for this project was generated and composed on the Macintosh. Color specifications to the printer were indicated on a tissue overlay, together with the exact silhouette for the die-cut stationery.

Many versions of the identity were created on the Macintosh before the final design was selected. On-screen editing and printout of an image is so easy that it was possible to view many more precisely rendered variations than would be feasible using traditional tools.

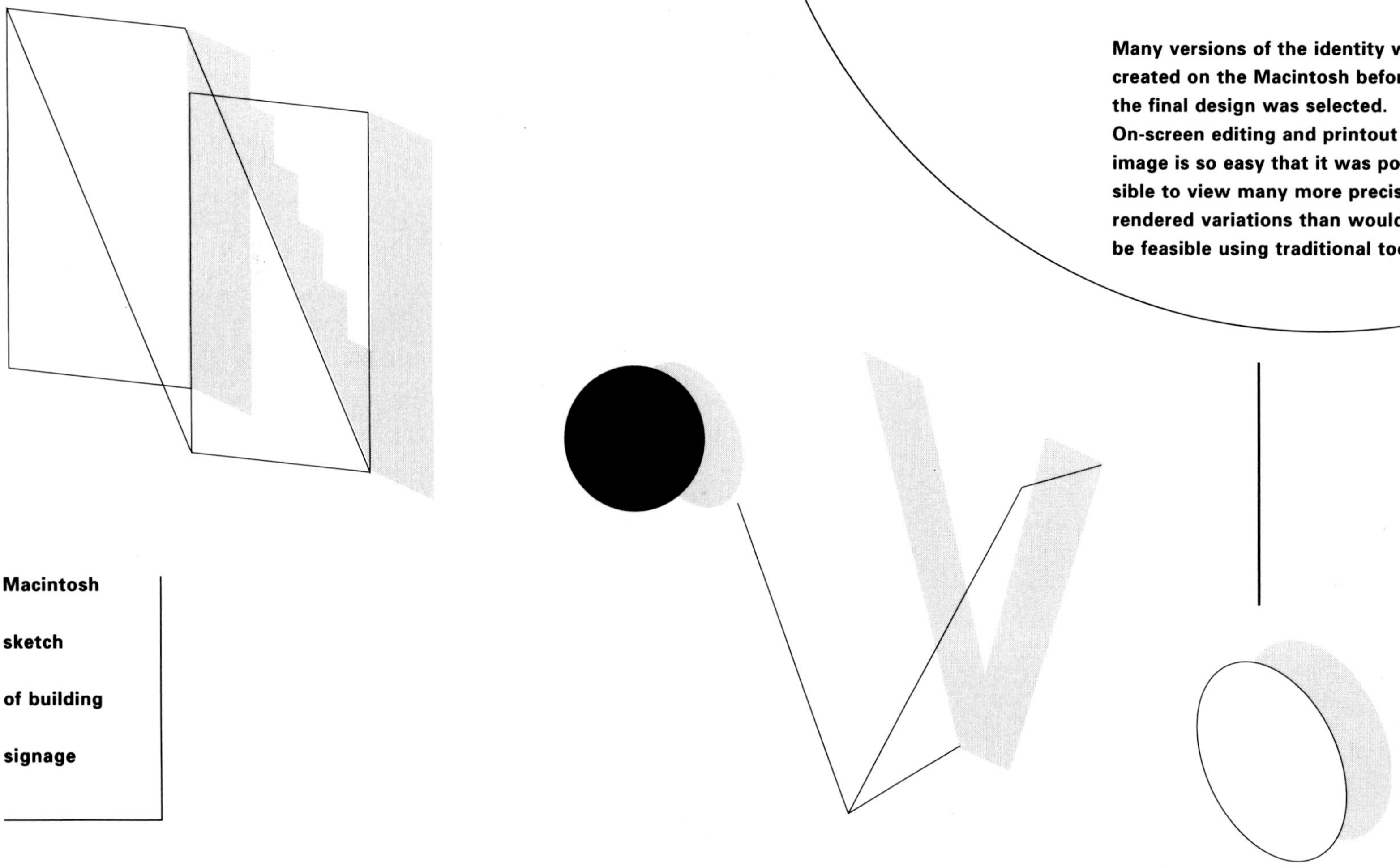

Macintosh

sketch

of building

signage

stilnovo

370 altara avenue

coral gables

florida 33146

305 441-9007

telex:
9102405248

fax: 305 441 1185

stilnovo

370 altara avenue   telex:
coral gables   9102405248
florida 33146
305 441-9007
fax: 305 441 1185

Postcard for store opening

Corporate identity and signage for Perloff / Webster; designers / developers.

The art for this project was generated and composed entirely on the Macintosh, and then sent to a Linotronic laser printer service for high-resolution output. The typefaces used were Univers and Emigre Matrix. The expanding range of type styles available on the Macintosh is rapidly reducing the amount of conventional typesetting ordered by the studio.

The resulting black and white 8 1 / 2" x 11" proofs of the identity were sent to the signmaker, with a tissue overlay to indicate color. He then used his own flatbed scanner to enlarge the proofs to the appropriate size in order to produce the on-site signage.

369-3688

P E R L O F F | WEBSTER

P E R L O F F | **WEBSTER**

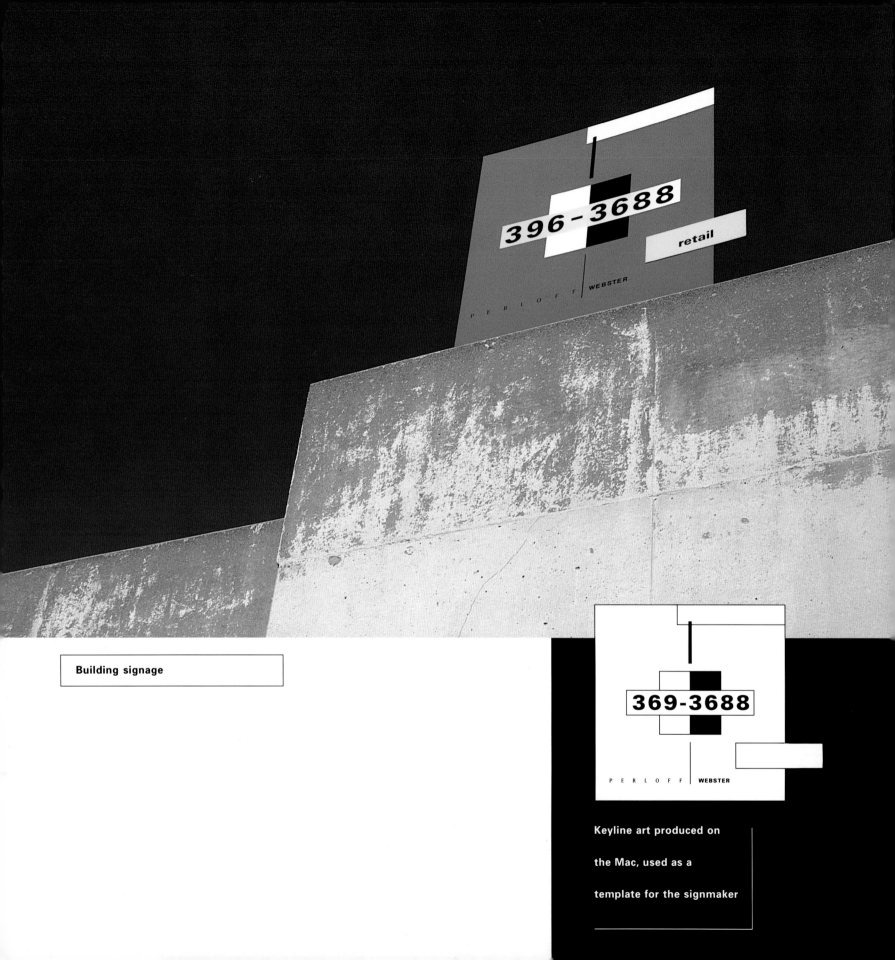

396-3688

retail

PERLOFF | WEBSTER

Building signage

369-3688

PERLOFF | WEBSTER

Keyline art produced on

the Mac, used as a

template for the signmaker

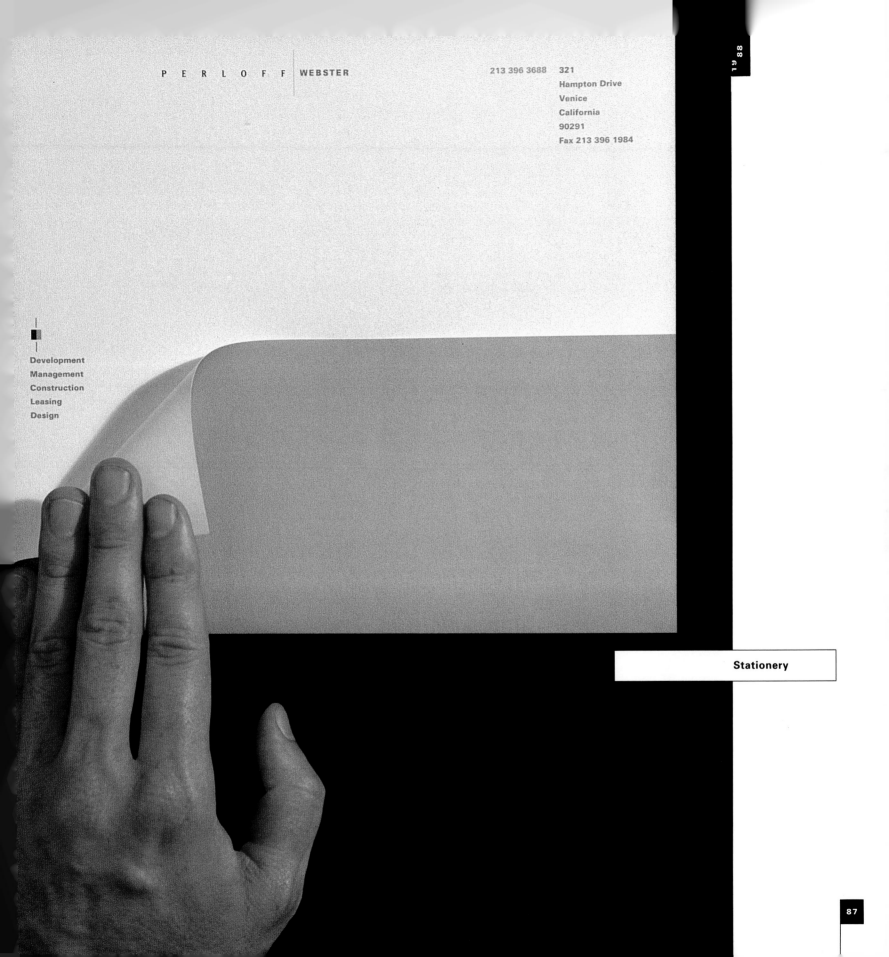

P E R L O F F | **WEBSTER**

213 396 3688   321
Hampton Drive
Venice
California
90291
Fax 213 396 1984

Development
Management
Construction
Leasing
Design

Stationery

liberty

A poster commissioned by the
French government to commemo-
rate the 200th anniversary of the
French Revolution.

Layered into this composition is a
negative photostat of the original
French "Declaration of the Rights of
Man," which was part of the original materials received by the studio.
The digitized images of a bird and
snake are intended to refer to their
symbolic roots—the snake standing
for transformation, the bird for
peace and freedom. These elements
are centered around a NASA col-
or transparency of the Earth as
seen from space. The yellow /
orange transition in the lower left
is a printer's gradation.

property

security

freedom

equality

The completed poster

April Greiman Los Angeles

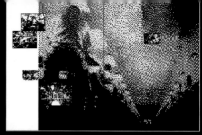
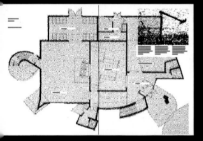

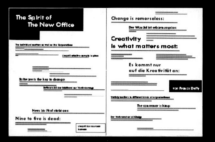
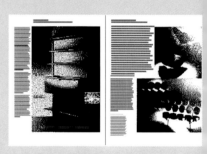

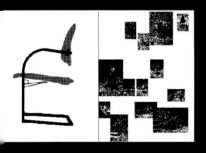

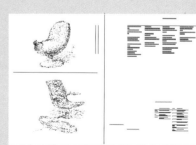
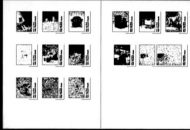

conic" first stage, sized to FAX, for client approval in Switzerland

An annual tabloid-size design magazine for Vitra.

Vitra is a Swiss company that manufactures classic contemporary office furniture, from vintage Charles Eames to the most recent high-tech Bellini chair. The magazine provides an eclectic and often playful feeling for the philosophy and spirit of Vitra as a whole.

The magazine layout and all the text was composed completely on the Macintosh, using PageMaker page composition software. The advantage of this approach, apart from cost, is flexibility. Many ideas can be precisely previsualized and corrected without delay, without leaving the studio.

A surprise in producing this initial miniature version was that I could see the whole magazine as a kind of iconic texture, free from detail. I kept this vision with me as a mental reminder of my original intuition for the overall visual structure of the piece.

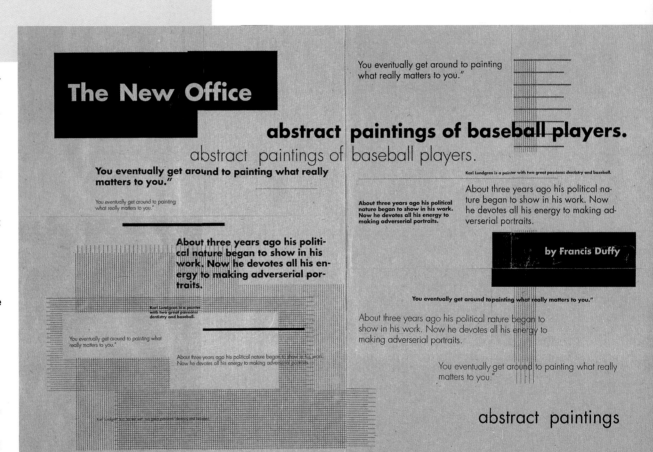

An original Kraft

paper concept

sketch for

client approval

The project went through three stages on the computer, using a rough-and-ready, full-size sketch for reference. The first was a post-card-sized mock-up with digitized versions of the illustrations, mostly "greek" (nonsense) text indications, and small hand-sketched color indications alongside, where appropriate. This mock-up was FAXed to the client overseas, and returned with comments.

Yelo grad?

inside front cover   1
table of contents

                    2 color printing

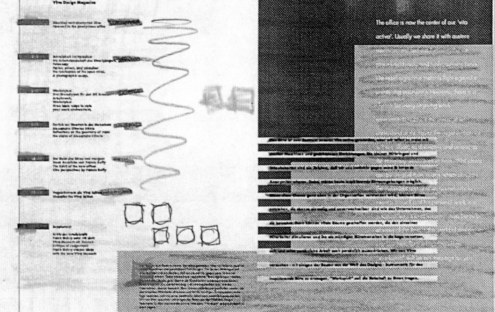

this page
has photo
credits

RF editorial
emphasis on German
and English

overprints screened
(light) photo of
phone lady

French text
starts here

photos of
Esprit,Chiat/Day
Holland Office start here (not shown) ↑

black + ~~*together*~~

"Iconic" first stage, with color indications for studio use

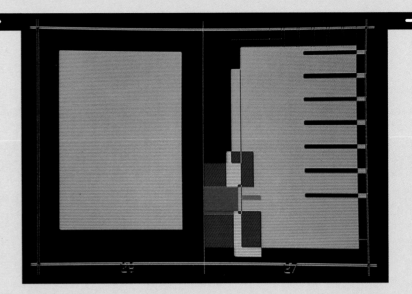

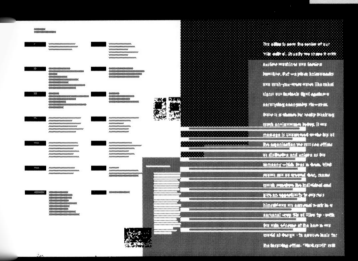

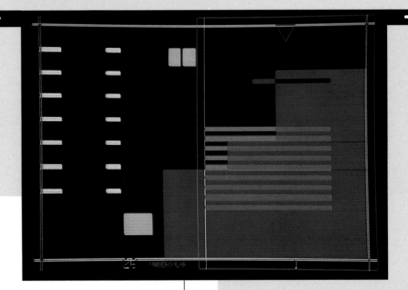

duced view of the

ond version of the page

nposition used as

guide for traditional

te-up at the third and

l stage

Computer screen view of

the printer's Gerber

System used to recon-

struct the paste-up of the

magazine into

lithographic film flats

Final offset printed pages

In theory, final page composition for the whole issue could have been created and printed out on the Mac (minus the illustrations), but the LaserWriter printer doesn't print tabloid-size pages. As a result, chunks of the composition were printed separately for the third and final version of the magazine and combined in a tabloid-size conventional paste-up.

The printer, in turn, reconstructed the underlying grid from the paste-up and restripped all the art according to their own (Gerber) system. This redundant step will soon be dropped when the Macintosh formally links to the high-end Gerber, Crossfield, and SciTex systems. When those connections are complete, a designer working with a desktop computer in the studio will be able to compose in the language of sophisticated equipment, without having to pay for it at that stage.

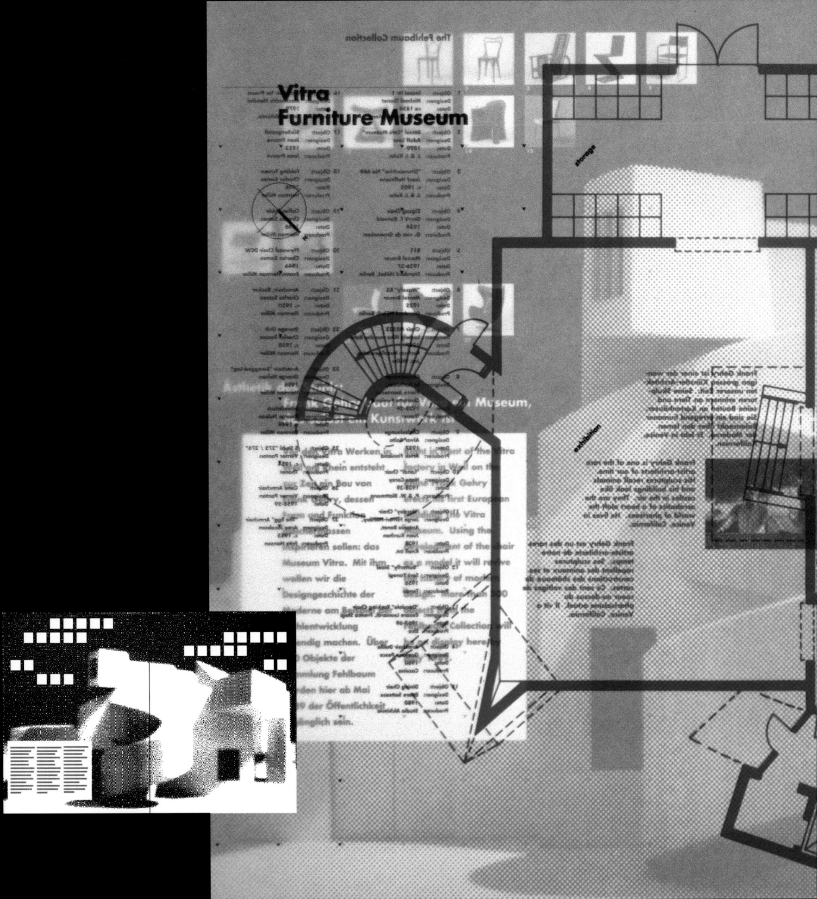

Vitra
Furniture Museum

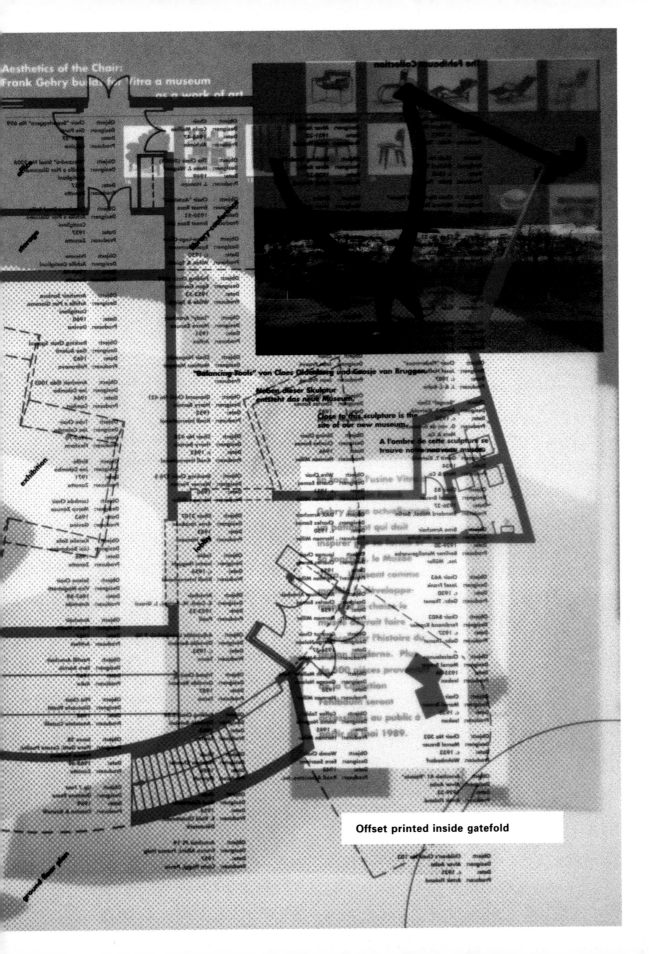

Offset printed inside gatefold

Drawings and photographs, some four color, were indicated on the layout for later inclusion in the conventional manner.

Digital halftone software isn't yet fine enough for studio purposes. In fact, this whole process illustrates the transitional nature of this technology, which will be the norm for the foreseeable future. Electronic technology continues to swallow traditional techniques at the low end, such as conventional typesetting, while it nibbles at new territory at the high end, such as color separation. The virtue of this evolution for the designer is that more and more of the process is moving to the design studio and away from third-party suppliers.

The second version, for studio use only, was created as an 8 1 / 2" x 11" printout, still using digitized versions of the illustrations, and the actual text (as opposed to "greek" type) as it came in. This tighter version gave an even better sense of what was becoming a dense and complex composition.

Sometimes I kept the bolder digitized versions of the illustrations that were originally intended only as indications of position on the layout (e.g., the toy robot on the cover), because I came to prefer them. Or I would even digitize a FAX of an illustration rather than use the illustration itself where the rougher texture seemed right.

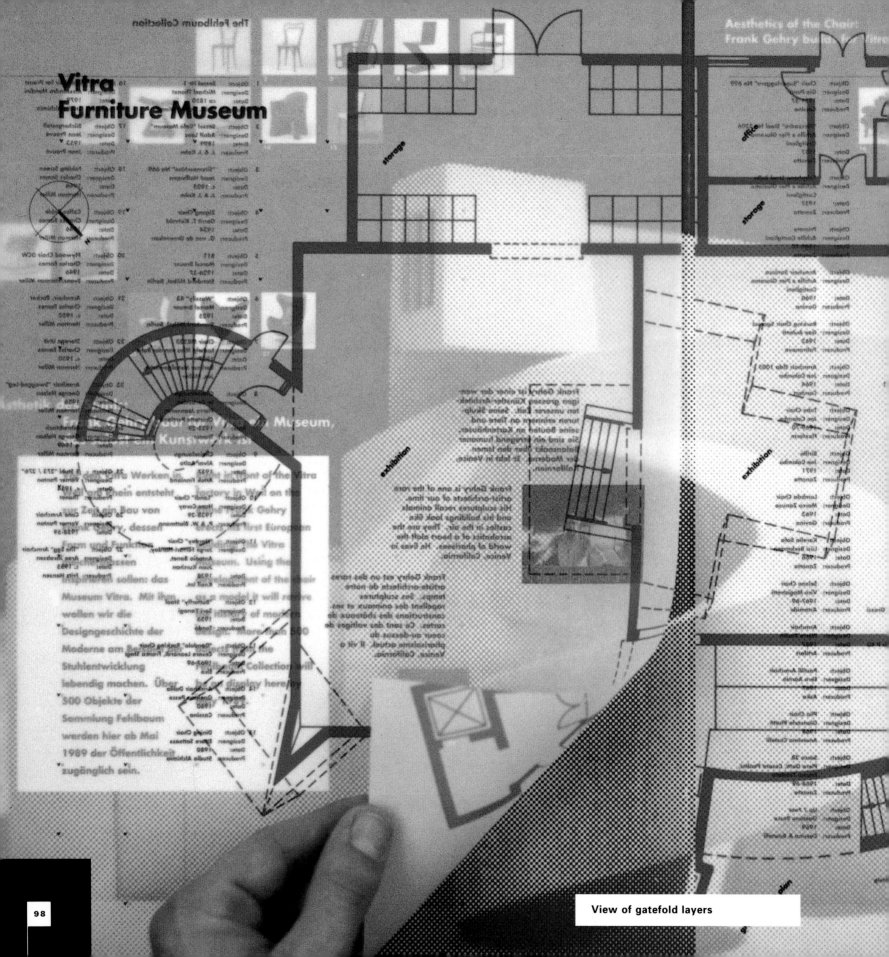

View of gatefold layers

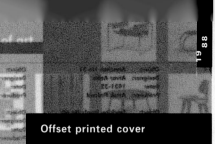

workspirit

Ray Eames
1916-1988

Museum Vitra

Premiere:
Citterios Stühle
The Chairs of Citterio
Les chaises de Citterio

Abschied vom anonymen Büro

Farewell to the Anonymous Office
Adieu au bureau anonyme

Workstyles: Drei Grundtypen

Workstyles: Three Basic Ways
Workstyles: Trois types élémentaires

Frank Gehry baut für Vitra

Frank Gehry builds for Vitra
Frank Gehry construit pour Vitra

Der Geist des Büros von morgen

The Spirit of the New Office
L'esprit du nouveau bureau

Come back, George Nelson!

Re-Editions of the Great Designer
Rééditions du grand designer

Gegen die Macht der Gewohnheit

Phantasy Power
Pouvoir de la fantaisie

Bellinissimo: Neue Gesichter

Bellinissimo: New Blood in the Family
Bellinissimo: Nouveaux visages

"We are the catalysts that transform the raw materials of the earth into energy. We are a continuation of the geologic process."

Diego Rivera

hybrid (hy'brid) **.n.** [L. *hybrida*, offspring of mixed parentage] **1**. the offspring produced by crossing two individuals of unlike genetic constitution; specif., the offspring of two animals or plants of different races, varieties, species, etc. **2**. anything of mixed origin, unlike parts, etc. **3**. *Linguis*. a word made up of elements from different languages, as *companionway* - **adj**. of, or having the nature of, a hybrid.

Hybrid Imagery

The idea of combining a variety of sources and techniques into individual compositions is a common characteristic of April Greiman Inc. This is especially true since the recent use of sophisticated Quantel Video and Graphic Paintboxes, which are similar to the Macintosh in image creation and editing, but with many additional sophisticated features.

Like the Macintosh, these Paintboxes are wonderful "editing engines" or "visual mixing valves" that permit the entering of imagery from still photographs, slides, drawings, and freeze-frames from video (live or prerecorded) into a stored library, ready to respond to the user. This library, together with the painting and image manipulation tools in the Paintboxes, become a powerful "light table of the mind," in which complex images may be built swiftly, recomposed, rethought, retouched, rejected, and refound. All this is accomplished on the screen, in front of you, immediately.

In the Paintbox environment you're able to see the entire layered composition as you work, as if it were final, as opposed to the traditional method in which gradations, overlays, type knockouts, and other processes are only indicated on layers of tissue, with a lot of complex guesswork involved. The outcome is often only visible in the printed result. The jump in the increase in subtlety of control is obvious, since the combined image is always visible in the electronic version as you go along. Also, the ability to build an electronic visual library creates a kind of personal image language which enhances imagination.

The Paintbox brings all tools together into a single new engine of graphic opportunity. Digital technology, whether Macintosh, Quantel, NeXT Inc., or something we haven't yet seen (but probably will), is simply an implosion, or "bursting inward" of separate image technologies into a common language, a single integrated creative environment.

A fundamentally new medium tends to be mistaken, at first, for the medium it appears to replace. For instance, photography was incorrectly thought to remove the necessity for painting; film was to replace theater; television was to replace film, and so on. None of this has happened.

It's also fascinating that a new tool may be invented which is almost perfectly designed for its ultimate purpose, which its inventors mistook. Edison thought the phonograph would be used primarily to play back vocally recorded letters. The discovery that motion pictures constituted a new form of narrative had to await artists who found that intercutting separate shots resulted in an entirely new kind of storytelling with an almost dreamlike power.

The same holds true for digital technologies. These aren't simply new tools for old tasks. They ask for a new kind of artist with an unconventional vision, combining ordinarily separate media into new hybrids, *ad hoc*. The age of the specialist is over. — EM

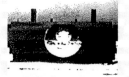

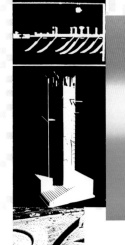

Southern California Institute of Architecture

This poster is for a lecture series at the Southern California Institute of Architecture. All text and imagery, with one exception, is produced on the computer, and pasted up conventionally.

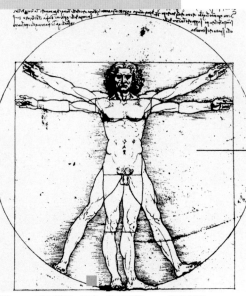

changing

concepts o

sci-

arc

in architect

and art

The image is a hybrid of five
processes:

• The Macintosh was used to produce:
all type and rules, the small images
on the edges (digitized from photographs), the overall orange coarse
digitized gradation, and the central
coarse digitized "ideal man."

• The smooth blue / yellow / red
gradation is from a library of images
generated on the Video Paintbox.
When I first heard about the Video
Paintbox, I rented time on it simply
for the experience and to generate a variety of very smooth color
gradations for unknown future uses.
This gradation was produced at least
a year before its appearance
on this poster.

• The central image of tumbled architectural elements (the exception
mentioned above) is a print from a
4" x 5" high-contrast black-and-
white negative of a steel engraving
of the work of the Baroque architect and scene designer, Pozzo.
The studio photostat camera also
shrank the small Mac-digitized images and blew up the overall orange
coarse gradation.

And, of course, the human hand produced the paste-up.

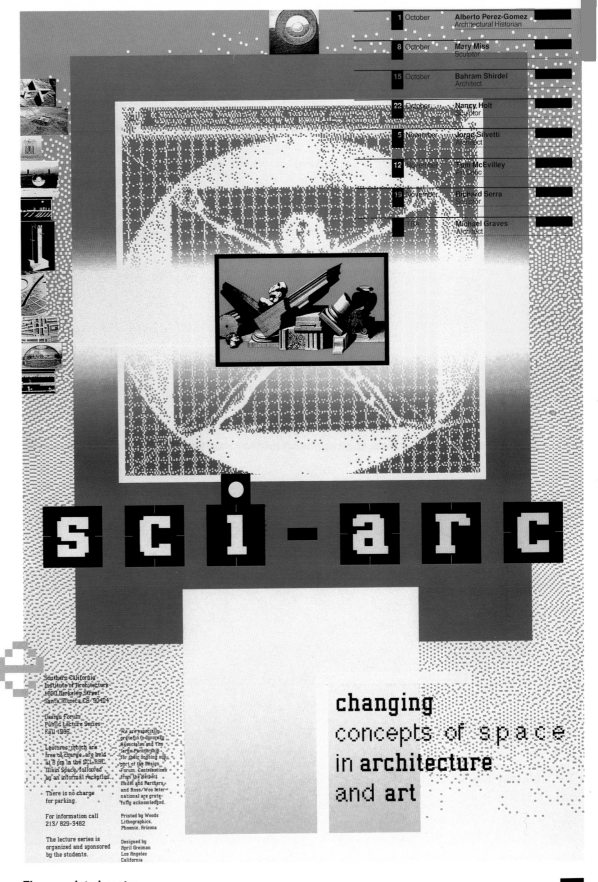

The completed poster

Inference Corporation

The Inference Corporation, a sophisticated artificial intelligence company, required a visual identity with several specialized applications.

Artificial intelligence software is intended to replace human personnel where the task requires intelligence to learn but little to execute. Monitoring hydraulic flow in a complex refinery, for instance, would be a typical candidate for an artificial intelligence application.

The basic typographic identity was produced by conventional means. Type was set and proofed, and the letterforms then subtly modified and letterspaced by hand.

Other applications involved more complex composite imagery. The software package sleeve combined gradations with a video texture

from my earliest video experiments at CalArts. The gradation itself employed an off-the-shelf Letraset gradation sheet which just happened to be at the right scale for the artwork. A red gradation was used in the paste-up (understood as the equivalent to black to the printer), and was ultimately printed in blue.

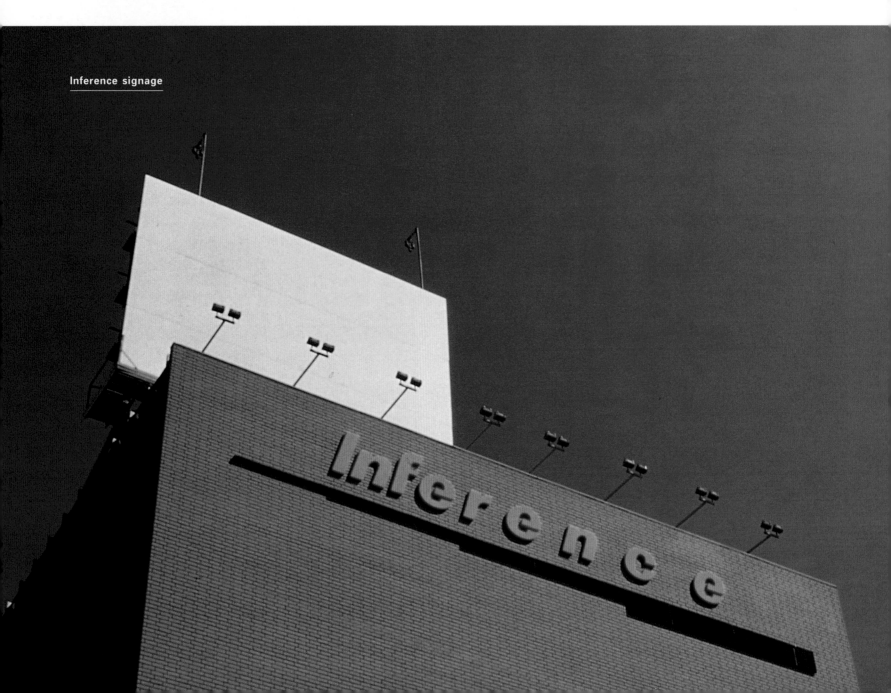

Inference signage

Packaging for Artificial Reasoning Tool (ART)

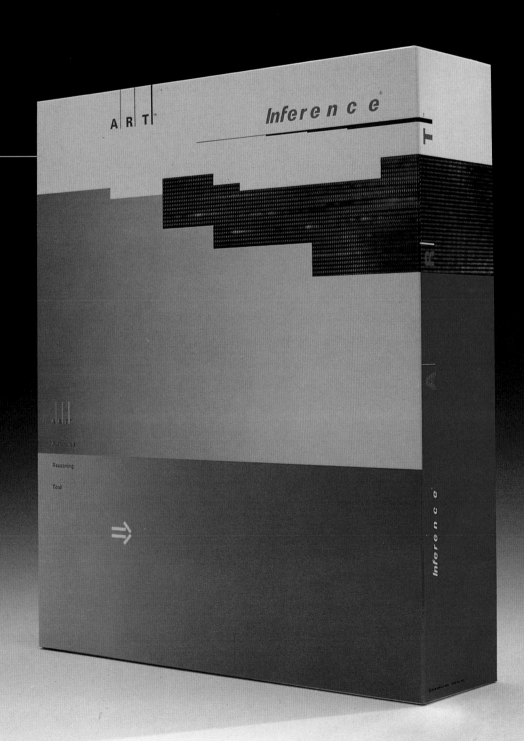

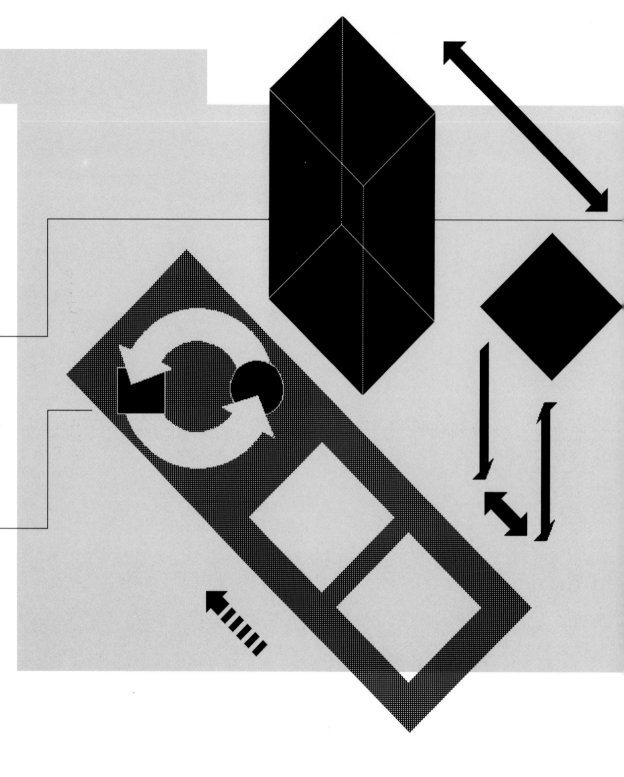

Inference diagrams
Collaboration with Eric Martin

The ambitious brochure explaining
the function of Inference software
was a real challenge. The original
materials relied on a lengthy,
difficult text to communicate the
nature of the product. To simplify
the materials, I suggested that
a series of computer-generated diagrams be created to replace much
of the verbiage.

The original idea was to build an
exact sketch of the basic structure
of the diagrams on the Macintosh,
using the printout as a visual guide
or reference for the Video Paintbox operator in constructing the
final images. It quickly became obvious that the process of translation
was taking much too long using this
approach, and a new Video Paintbox
appointment was scheduled.

That same evening, the Macintosh
reference images were redrawn
as black-and-white silhouettes of
the separate elements of the diagram to speed the translation process. The following day they were
scanned into the Video Paintbox
by a video camera, then simply assembled and colorized on screen,
a much faster and more economical
process. This left time to fine tune
what the Video Paintbox does best,
such as adjusting the degree of
transparency of one layer over another and the relative color balance
among the elements. Though
this was a spontaneous hybrid of
desktop and sophisticated technology, it is increasingly becoming
the case that desktop tools are
being formally linked to expensive,
powerful "visual composers."

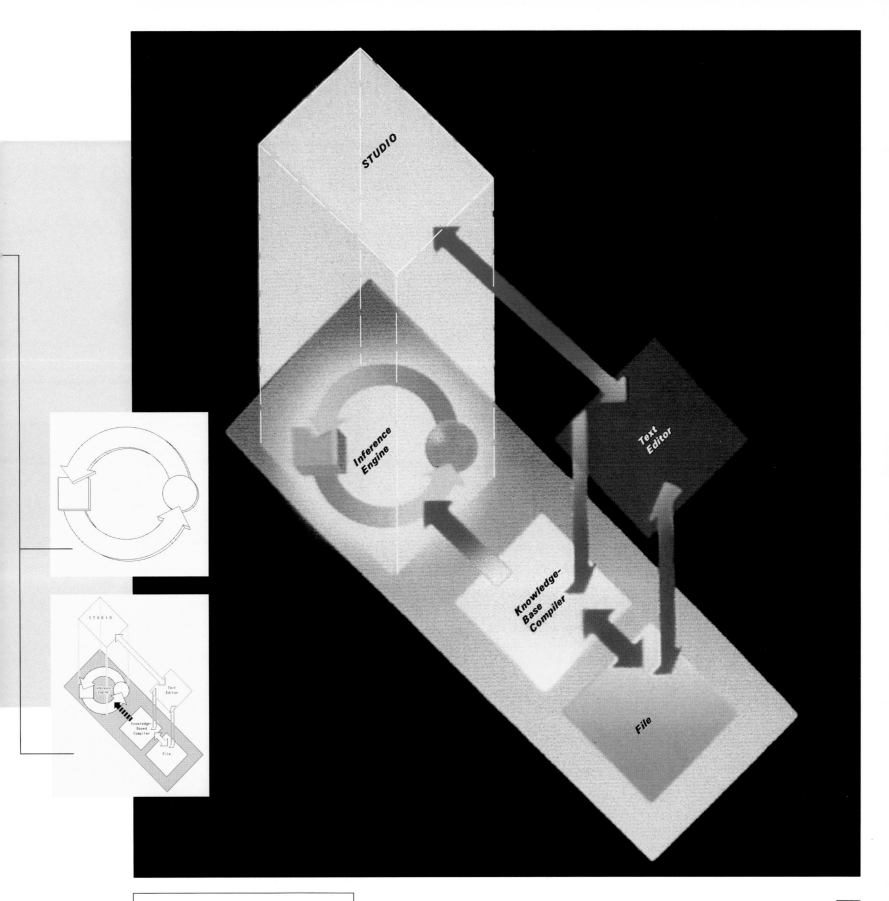

STUDIO

Inference
Engine

Text
Editor

Knowledge-
Base
Compiler

File

STUDIO

Inference
Engine

Text
Editor

Knowledge-
Based
Compiler

File

The completed electronic diagram

A cover for *PC World* magazine, featuring the graphic capabilities of IBM-type personal computers.

The irony is that the cover image was not produced with IBM technology but with the Video Paintbox and the Macintosh.

Several black-and-white graphic elements were scanned into the Video Paintbox by a video camera:

• A photograph of clouds, which forms the background, and a photostat of hieroglyphics.

• A Macintosh printout of the digitized eye, hand, ball, and the 3-D bars and pie chart.

The large letter "B" was generated from the Video Paintbox type library and colorized using its paint tools, as were all the other elements entered via the video camera. For example, a complex Video Paintbox gradation was layered into the background cloud photo so that the original black in the image was replaced by a subtle diagonal yellow / orange / green / blue gradation. This effect was achieved by simply swapping the color gradation for any instance of black in the cloud layer with the push of a Video Paintbox button.

In the actual publication, this image was overlaid by the *PC World* masthead and feature headlines, thus disguising its origins.

The completed

image prior

to the application

of type

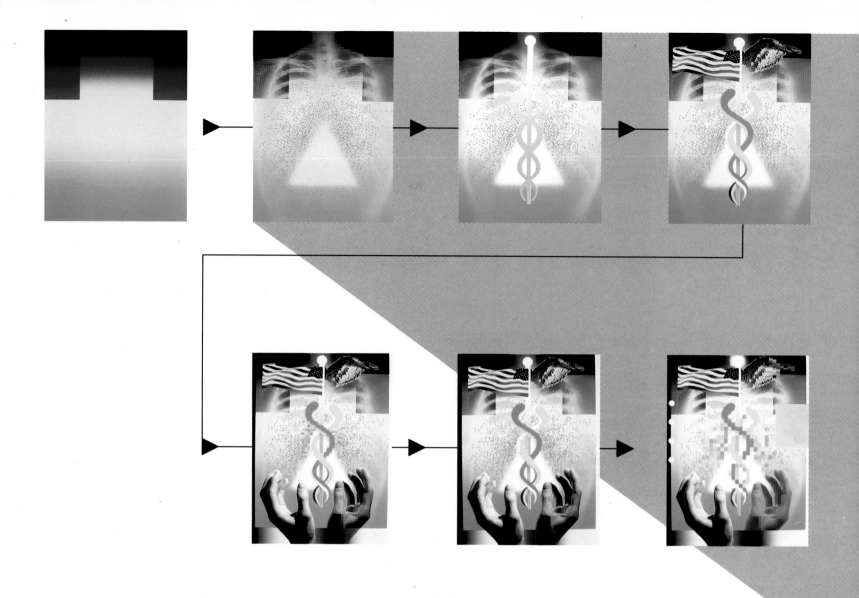

Shaping the Future of Healthcare

A poster announcing the health-care
symposium, "Shaping the Future of Health Care."

The completed poster

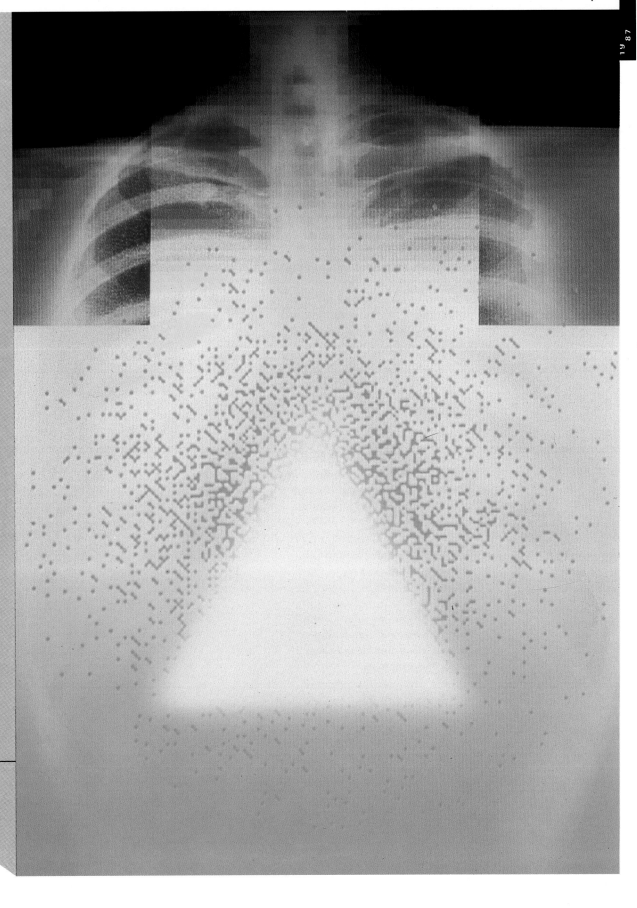

This was my first attempt to apply the Quantel Video Paintbox to an actual commission. It was instructive to me, in retrospect.

I understood that the Video Paintbox could accept images from a wide variety of sources. Images I brought to the session included: a chest X-ray negative; photographs of a flag and an eagle; and a drawing of a caduceus (the ancient symbol for the medical profession). The hands were video clips of the hands of one of the studio designers, shot live in the Video Paintbox facility. The Video Paintbox itself was used to create the gradations, image manipulation (notice the "mosaicizing" of the caduceus, a Video Paintbox effect), and composition.

While the experience of creating the image was exhilarating, it's fair to say that the hypnotic effect of the process of layering encouraged an overly complicated result. The sheer ease with which combinations may be tried, tuned, and rethought on the spot can lead to an overstuffed feeling until you get your balance. Looking back, I feel that a much earlier stage in the layering process was probably the place to stop.

Workspace '87

A poster announcing an annual
San Francisco convention /
symposium on office furniture
and interiors.

This Video Paintbox composition
combines many sources and techniques into a single complex image:

- The city image is from an 11" x 14"
  color print of a photograph of central San Francisco. It was scanned
  into the Video Paintbox, with
  the right half altered by the "mosaicizing" tool, breaking that part
  of the image into a blocky pattern
  of squares.

- The eye is a live video freeze-
  frame, shot in the studio. It was
  placed into the Video Paintbox composition and then tipped. The blue
  of the iris was intensified with the
  paint tools.

- The hand and ball combination
  is from the studio library of digitized
  Macintosh images.

- The blue chair, originally a Macintosh line drawing, was shaded,
  colored, sized, and tipped using
  Video Paintbox tools.

Keyline artwork,

used to

prepare the

accompanying

brochure

- On the left-hand side, the sun and its rays were drawn by hand. Beneath lies a scanned-in coarse halftone of a cloud photograph, printed in blue over a yellow-to-white Video Paintbox gradation. The result is a green-to-blue transition for the cloud area as a whole.

- The right-hand red gradation was generated by hand with an airbrush.

- All the text was produced traditionally, with hand and photo techniques employed to distort it. In hindsight, I feel that the composition fails to come together as a single gesture because of the type handling. It appears not to work strongly enough with the image as a whole. If Video Paintbox typography were more sophisticated it would have helped. And this may soon be the case.

The completed poster

A cover for the 1988 American Institute of Graphic Arts Annual.

water

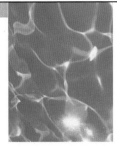

sand

clouds

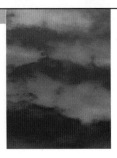

This cover gave me my first opportunity to use the more recent Quantel Graphic Paintbox. The Quantel Video Paintbox was designed to produce art for television, even though I've used it to produce art for print by shooting off the screen. The more recent Graphic Paintbox, however, a completely digital machine, is specifically designed to produce art for print as final product, automatically producing color separation art from the finished screen composition.

The Graphic Paintbox uses a Sony HDTV monitor which doubles the resolution of the Video Paintbox, yielding an image which at first glance seems as sharp as a magazine page. It also gives the artist unique control over how a color is defined and ultimately seen in print—in ways which exceed conventional print technology in clarity of hue, saturation, and brightness.

For example, the yellow component of the AIGA cover image gradation is pure yellow, not mixed with other hues, as would ordinarily be the case with a traditional printer's gradation seen close up. Or if you indicate that an area should be 100 percent white, the ultimate film image sent to the printer will be completely clear in that area, i.e., transparent to the white of the paper. This is great for tight control.

To produce this design, the three color slides of the source images were digitized by a slide scanner and entered into the Graphic

Paintbox library of images. Then they were brought up, one by one, and cropped, sized, and composed together on the screen. The rear gradation was separately produced on the Graphic Paintbox and added to the image. The white "water" highlight was added to the evolving composition using the Graphic Paintbox "airbrush" tool.

Once complete, a linked "digital frame recorder" electronically translated the digitally generated image on screen back into a 4" x 5" color transparency which was then given to the printer for traditional separation, platemaking, and printing. Interestingly, the process began by translating color slides into digital form for composition, and ended with retranslation of the digital composition back into a color slide, followed by the conventional four-color printing process.

The typography was also produced conventionally, then separately positioned on a tissue in relation to a color stat from the color slide of the Graphic Paintbox image. Why? The reasons were simple: the range of typefaces then available in the Graphic Paintbox type library was inadequate, as well as the cumbersome custom control over letterspacing (at $500 / hr.). Another factor was that the resolution of the Graphic Paintbox, while spectacular by video standards, still cannot do justice to the exacting subtlety of classic letterforms. It's ironic, since the near future of this technology may exceed photography in sharpness.

In a sense I'm ambivalent about the high quality of Graphic Paintbox imagery. On the one hand it makes possible elaborate, subtle image composition in **real time**. No more crossing your fingers while you wait for proofs. On the other hand, I still enjoy the lower resolution Video Paintbox for certain purposes, precisely because it shows the grain or texture of video.

This is an important point. To me, texture is equivalent to emotion. The more texture, the more I evoke emotional response. High resolution for its own sake is meaningless. It is too perfect, too seamless. It rejects feeling, the way chrome reflects light. I like to show the process behind what you see.

Of course, since the Graphic Paintbox accepts all forms of input, including imagery generated on the Video Paintbox, it's possible to combine the feeling of several processes or textures interacting when you want.

A big limitation to both the Video and Graphic Paintboxes is cost— several hundreds of thousands to own, hundreds per hour to rent. And you must develop a good working relationship with an operator. At the same time, what costs hundreds of thousands today will cost only thousands tomorrow. And, you'll be able to run it yourself. In fact, certain applications on desktop computers are beginning to equal these sophisticated Paintbox capabilities.

GRAPHIC DESIGN U S A : 8

1987

THE ANNUAL OF THE AMERICAN INSTITUTE OF GRAPHIC ARTS

The completed cover

Extreme close-up
of the laser-produced
billboard version,
in which the effect
of the separate
primary color spray-
guns, which produce
the image, is
clearly visible. The
"dot-and-streak"
quality to the individ-
ual points of color
reflects the scanning
process itself; we
are literally capturing
"light in motion" —
a moving pointillist
painting.

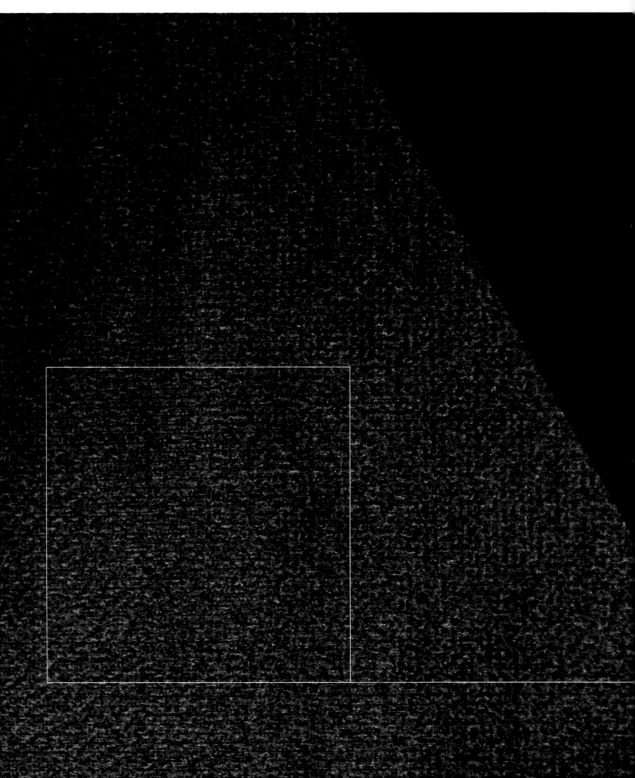

What begins as one object may, surprisingly, become another in the digital process. I discovered, for example, that the same disk which stored my AIGA image could also be output on the new Metromedia laser-scan billboard engine—capable of producing a large blowup of an image up to 20' x 60'. As a gesture, Metromedia produced a (14' x 20') version of the cover for the annual meeting of the AIGA, which now hangs in the studio.

National Endowment for the Arts

Work produced for an individual grant using new technology.

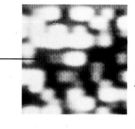

A grant from the National Endowment for the Arts gave me an opportunity to freely explore the Graphic Paintbox without a specific object in mind. Since this medium is so fluid and spontaneous, it's difficult now to describe exactly what is happening at any point in the process I followed. Roughly, here are some of the elements that were used in that process:

The black Chinese character was scanned in, and is echoed by a yellow negative of the form created with the Graphic Paintbox airbrush. The red ellipse was also airbrushed in the same manner. Laser-scans of a color slide of water form the tubular shapes in which the color has been oddly intensified using Graphic Paintbox controls. Part of the general background is a Macintosh gradation, against which is placed a ribbon of scanned-in

cloud imagery. The floating parallelogram was edited on the Graphic Paintbox from the studio library of color transparencies of manipulated video landscapes. The yellow circle with the line emerging from it was also created on the Graphic Paintbox. This eclectic mixture of techniques is typical of the composition as a whole.

Though there is no particular end or goal to this exercise, the ambiguous, mysterious feel of the evolving image is unique to this new medium, with a hybrid texture all its own.

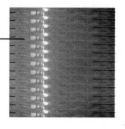

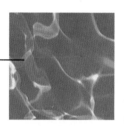

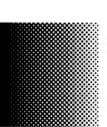

Slide sequence

documenting th

work as it pro-

gressed, commu

cating the liquid

quality of the

process, the eas

with which trans

formations may

occur, and the w

in which separat

elements may

be composed ar

recomposed usi

simple comman

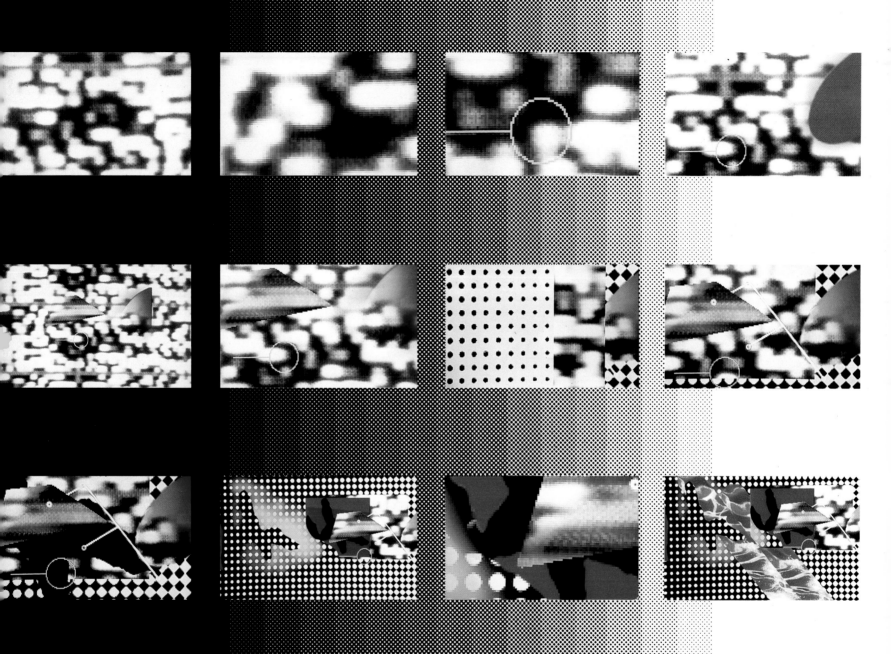

A composite image from the process

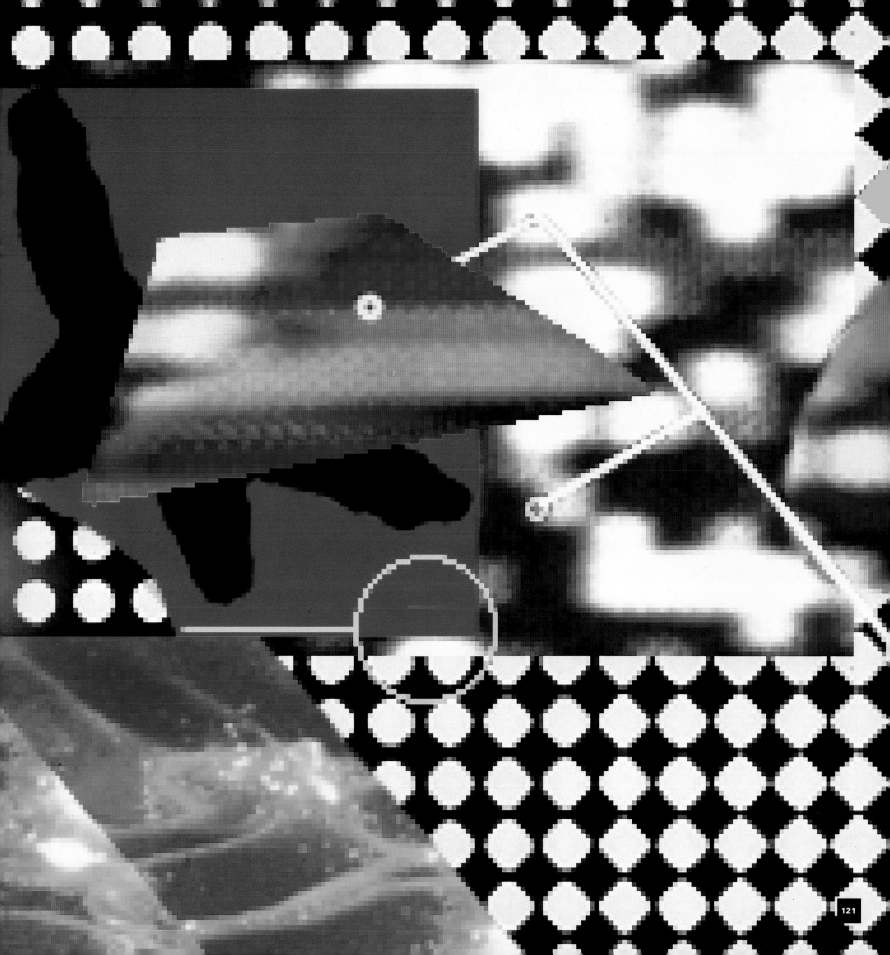

"t.v. is the new

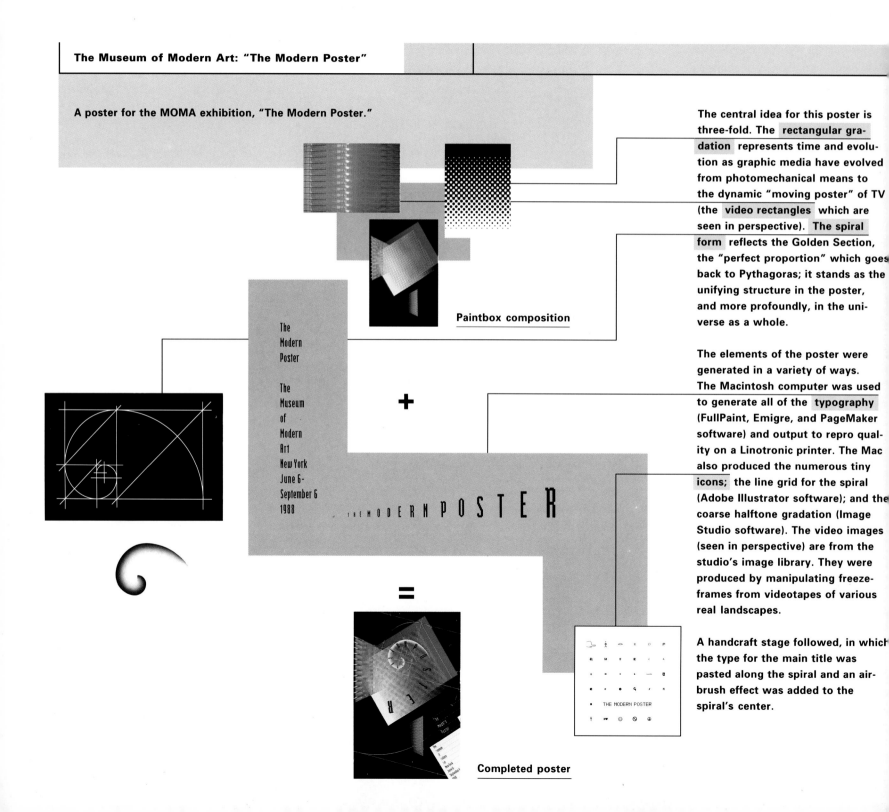

The Museum of Modern Art: "The Modern Poster"

A poster for the MOMA exhibition, "The Modern Poster."

Paintbox composition

The Modern Poster

The Museum of Modern Art New York June 6- September 6 1988

+

=

Completed poster

The central idea for this poster is three-fold. The rectangular gradation represents time and evolution as graphic media have evolved from photomechanical means to the dynamic "moving poster" of TV (the video rectangles which are seen in perspective). The spiral form reflects the Golden Section, the "perfect proportion" which goes back to Pythagoras; it stands as the unifying structure in the poster, and more profoundly, in the universe as a whole.

The elements of the poster were generated in a variety of ways. The Macintosh computer was used to generate all of the typography (FullPaint, Emigre, and PageMaker software) and output to repro quality on a Linotronic printer. The Mac also produced the numerous tiny icons; the line grid for the spiral (Adobe Illustrator software); and the coarse halftone gradation (Image Studio software). The video images (seen in perspective) are from the studio's image library. They were produced by manipulating freeze-frames from videotapes of various real landscapes.

A handcraft stage followed, in which the type for the main title was pasted along the spiral and an airbrush effect was added to the spiral's center.

poster

Original video landscape

Original manipulated video image

Macintosh gradation

Color slides shot
during the original
manipulation of
the video landscapes
were laser-scanned
and entered into
the Graphic Paintbox
as a library of images
with which to work.
The bottom row
includes images for
other projects.
Individual images were
selected and brought
to the screen for
retouching or editing
with other compo-
nents of the electronic
composition.

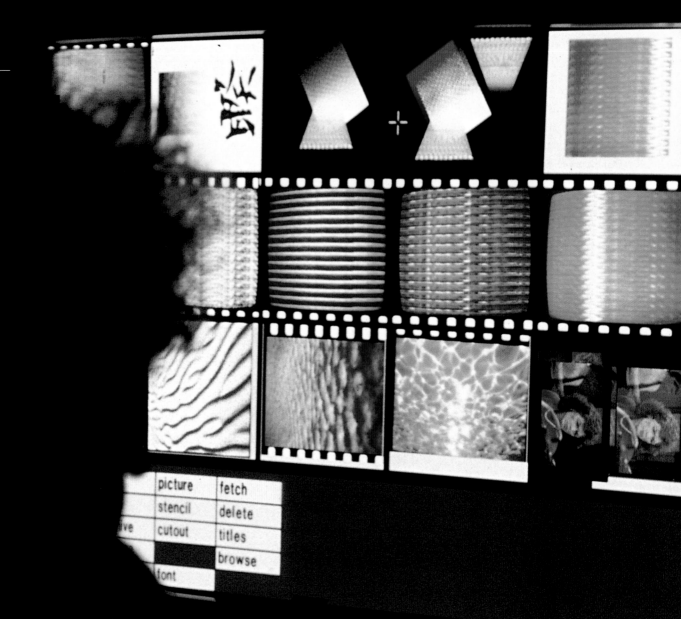

To produce the composition, several steps were involved:

First the video images were put into perspective using the Video Paintbox. These images, as well as the coarse dot gradation produced on the Macintosh, were then laser-scanned into a Quantel Graphic Paintbox where they were then manipulated into position on its high-resolution screen. Additional effects were introduced using Graphic Paintbox tools, such as the vanishing transparency effects of the video images, the feathered edge and the "mosaicizing" of the upper left video image, as well as the copying, flipping, colorizing, and positioning of the overlaid dot gradations. This composite image was then output to an 8" x 10" color transparency.

The final comp for the client was produced by hand, combining a color stat of the Graphic Paintbox image with the type, small icons, spiral, and airbrush elements generated at the studio. Some further retouching and masking by hand of the Graphic Paintbox image occurred at this stage as well, necessitating another session on the Graphic Paintbox after the comp was approved so that those changes could be entered into the original electronic composite.

The printer received the final 8" x 10" Graphic Paintbox transparency along with a single board of associated line art (type, spiral, etc.) paste-up.

Original Paintbox composition

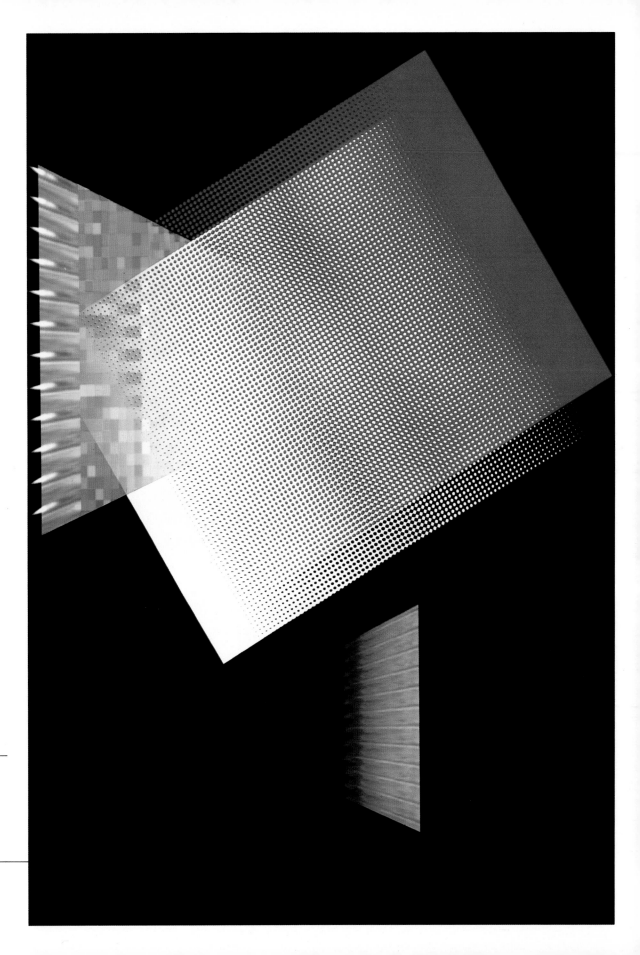

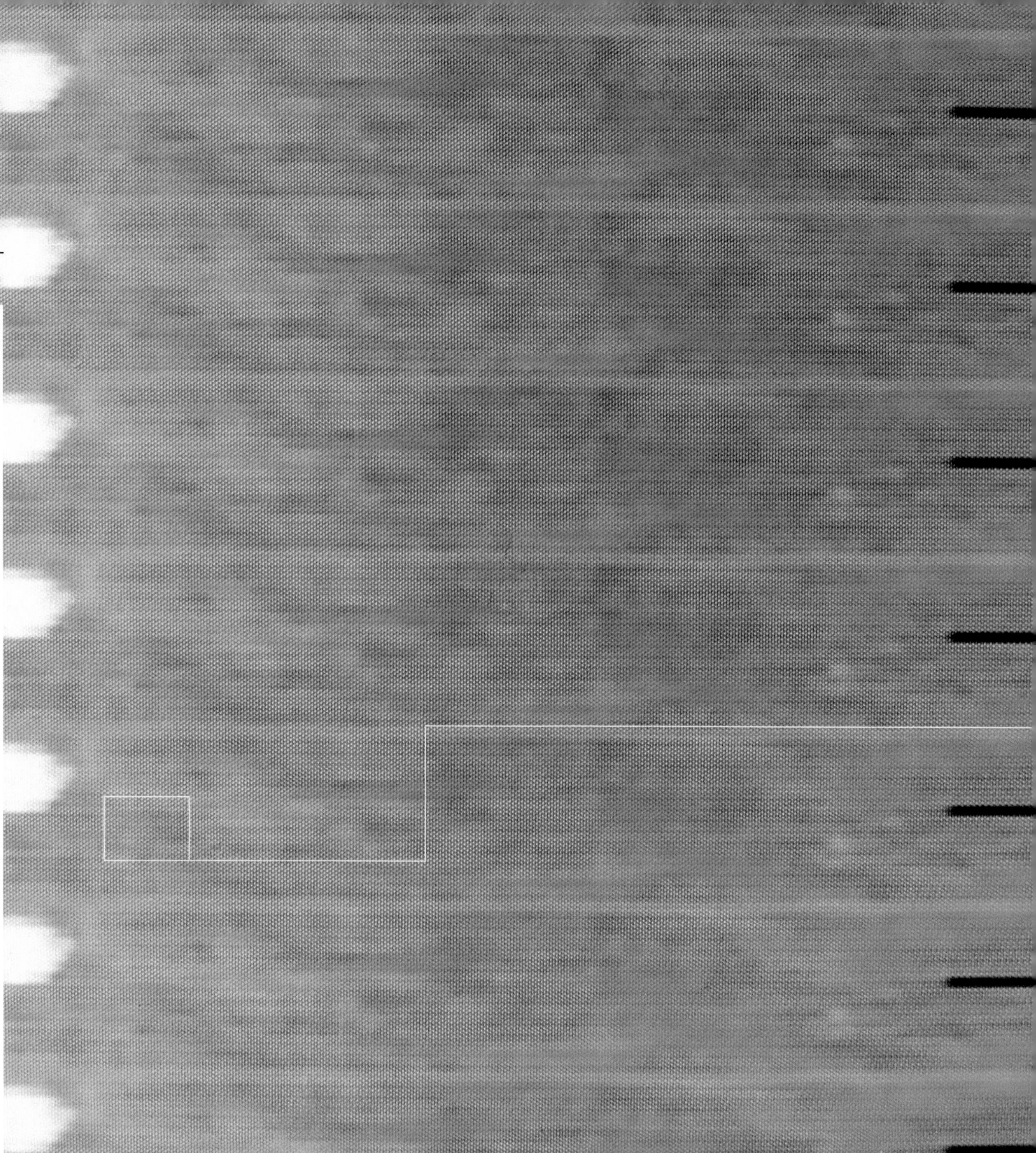

Sections of the image
were magnified and
painstakingly retouched,
often through creating a
mask and then applying
the Graphic Paintbox
version of an airbrush to
smoothly recolor or
recontour. In this way
subtle manipulations,
often impossible to
previsualize using
conventional tools, can
be seen and edited in
real time, such as effects
of degree of layering
transparency or control
of color transitions.

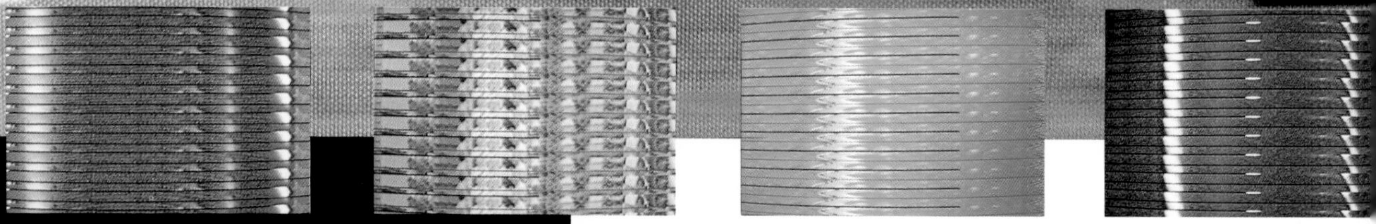

Out-takes from video manipulation session

The integration
of hand
and electronic
technique;
printout of type
generated on
the computer is
positioned in
the traditional
manner.

The type image
is brought into
the composition
as a whole

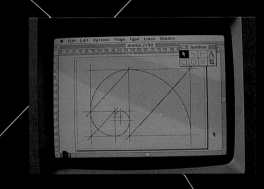

THE MODERN POSTER

THE MODERN POSTER

This roster of generic icons

from history was created

on the Macintosh

and greatly reduced photo-

graphically, then added

to the paste-up as mini-

atures to be discovered by

the discerning viewer.

The completed poster

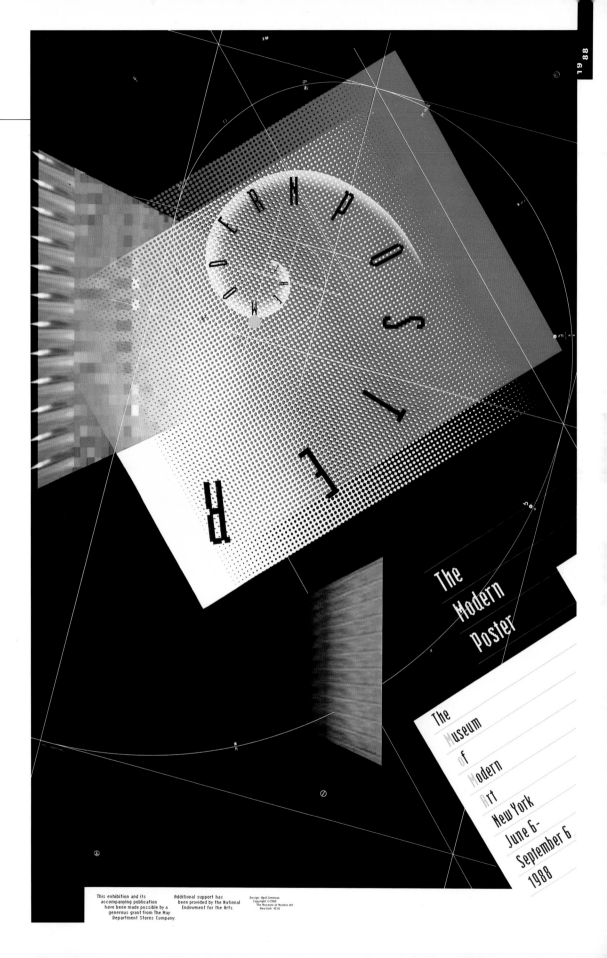

The Cycle of Discovery

The work in progress at April Greiman Inc reflects the impact of new technology on the traditional design process. What's become obvious is that new techniques typically overlap rather than replace old techniques. Certain traditional methods seem to be timeless. It's just the balance that changes. In fact, the tools that become obsolete the quickest are prior versions of recently upgraded digital hardware and software.

The transition from photomechanical to digital formats is a gradual one, however abrupt or disorienting it may seem at any given moment as it evolves. This means that there is no "right" time to enter the digital stream. Any time is as good as any other. It's not a particular product which you are deciding to buy but an ever-transforming process that you decide to join.

For the studio, this process is continuous:

Layering

Taking print technology to the limit; diverse image sources; collaging; two-dimensional into three-dimensional; gesture; metaphorical space and movement.

Hybridizing

Environmental design; video imagery; computer image / text / production process; the integration of textures; FAX, modem; joining the communications web.

The next stages:

Interactivity

The "responsive" graphic object; from implicit to explicit dialogue. The incorporation of real sound and movement. The screen as well as print as output.

The "wholographic" environment

A tentative Greiman studio term for a practical and poetic unity transcending old structures. Simultaneity replacing sequence, separation, and hierarchy. A new global language. A new global culture.

All media are collapsing into a common language or common digital toolkit. At the same time, the world is suddenly being made small, suddenly unified by the global electronic network. New paradigms replace the old.

What is important to realize is that sophisticated capability is coming to the desktop, with all the conceptual challenge and opportunity that that brings. Sophistication, in this world, has less to do with budgets than with ideas. — EM

Cerritos Performing Arts Center

The design of exterior tile patterns
for a large performing arts center,
for the architect, Barton Myers.

Color palette

The process began with color sketches in cut Color-Aid and PMS paper. Once basic color relationships and patterns were developed using this traditional technique, the collages were then directly scanned into the Macintosh and further developed as larger repeated black-and-white textures. At a certain point, the basic black-and-white pattern modules were re-created and refined in Image Studio, a retouching program.

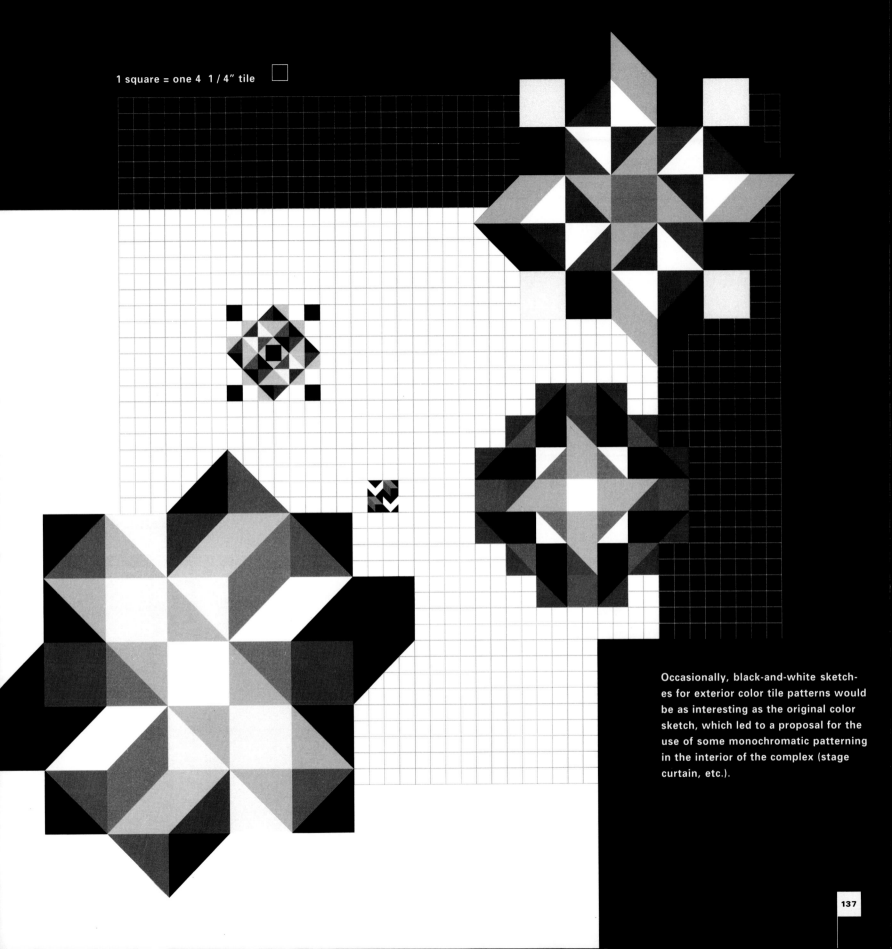

1 square = one 4 1/4" tile

Occasionally, black-and-white sketches for exterior color tile patterns would be as interesting as the original color sketch, which led to a proposal for the use of some monochromatic patterning in the interior of the complex (stage curtain, etc.).

137

The architect's working model

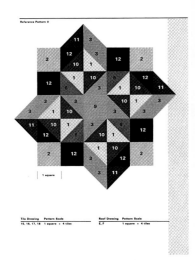

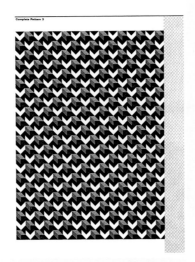

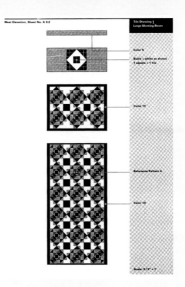

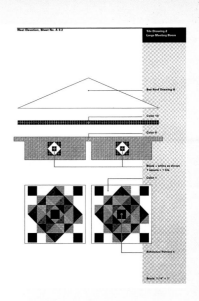

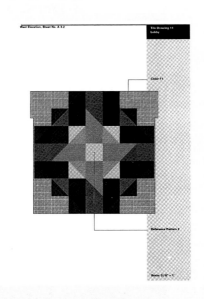

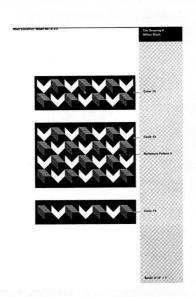

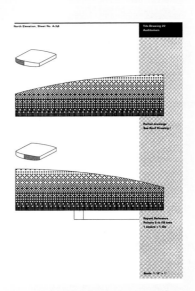

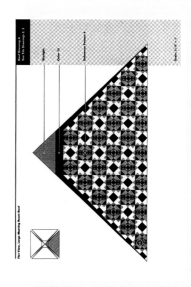

A specifications booklet for the tile patterns was also created on the Macintosh to accompany the architectural specifications sent to bidders.

TSE Cashmere

A new name and graphic system for a California clothing company using cashmere from China, originally called Cashmere Concepts. "Tse" (pronounced "say") is the name of one of the company's owners.

The graphic solution blends an Asian or calligraphic feeling with the simplicity of computer generation. The Macintosh was used for all applications, from the identity to the basic "line list," or up-to-date listing of products for trade shows.

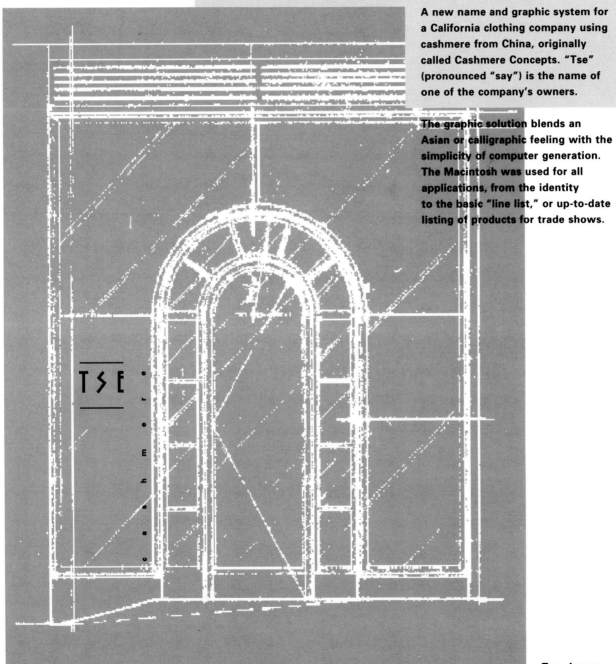

Tse signage

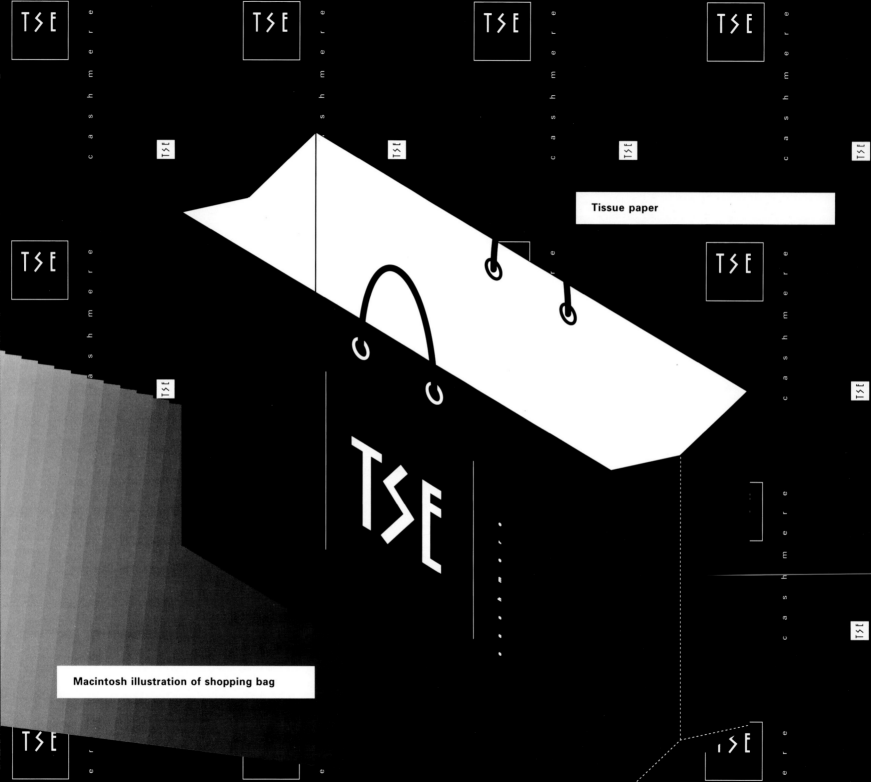

Tissue paper

Macintosh illustration of shopping bag

ONE HUNDRED DOLLAR GIFT CERTIFICATE

Date

To   From

T ϟ E   cashmere $100

Gift certificate

143

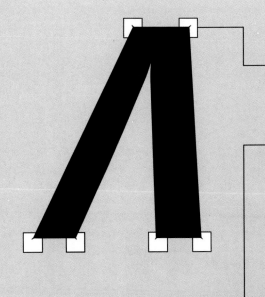

A graphic program for a new golf club in Japan.

Affiliation with a golf club confers prestige and provides a luxurious and relaxed setting for corporate social life in Japan. This program for a new club (for the architectural firm, Morphosis) extends to shop, signage, restaurant, and object design in the complex.

The central symbol is a fusion of "golf ball" and "rising sun," which sounds odd in print but seems to work as an image. It was created in Adobe Illustrator software, where the subtle control of shapes and groups of shapes encourages extensive fine tuning.

The type identity originated as high-resolution (Linotronic) output set in the Macintosh Univers font. The letterform designer, Leah Hoffmitz, then altered letter weight and spacing by hand, including the addition of "tick marks" to letter corners for the smaller sizes, to retain crispness in reduction. Fine control of letterforms is important to an identity that will vary widely in its application.

I composed these elements in the spirit of typographic and symbolic "landscape," in which the size of the symbol represents distance, and therefore time.

J   A   P   A   N

PGA
Golf Club

Bellini Office Furniture

A brochure for the Bellini line for the
Vitra furniture company.

Work on the Bellini brochure is
similar to the *Workspirit* magazine
project in method and approach,
but smoother. In both, Vitra has
been involved at every stage of
design, even though thousands of
miles away. The studio's digital
page production approach and FAX
communication system has become
almost second nature, easily bridg-
ing the physical distance between
Los Angeles and this Swiss client.

Creating scanned art for roughs,
and even some final art, has
become easier since we traded our
video digitizing technique for a
flatbed scanner as a means of
entering images.

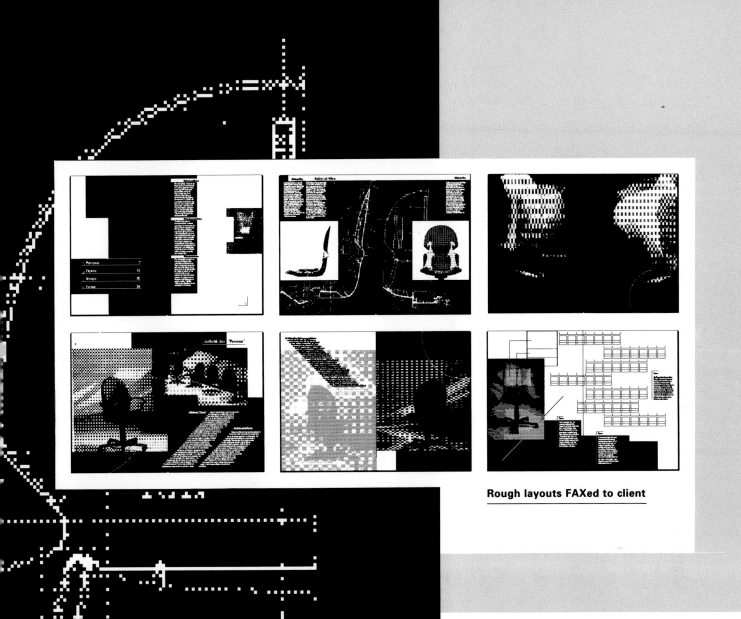

Rough layouts FAXed to client

Scanned illustration used as final art

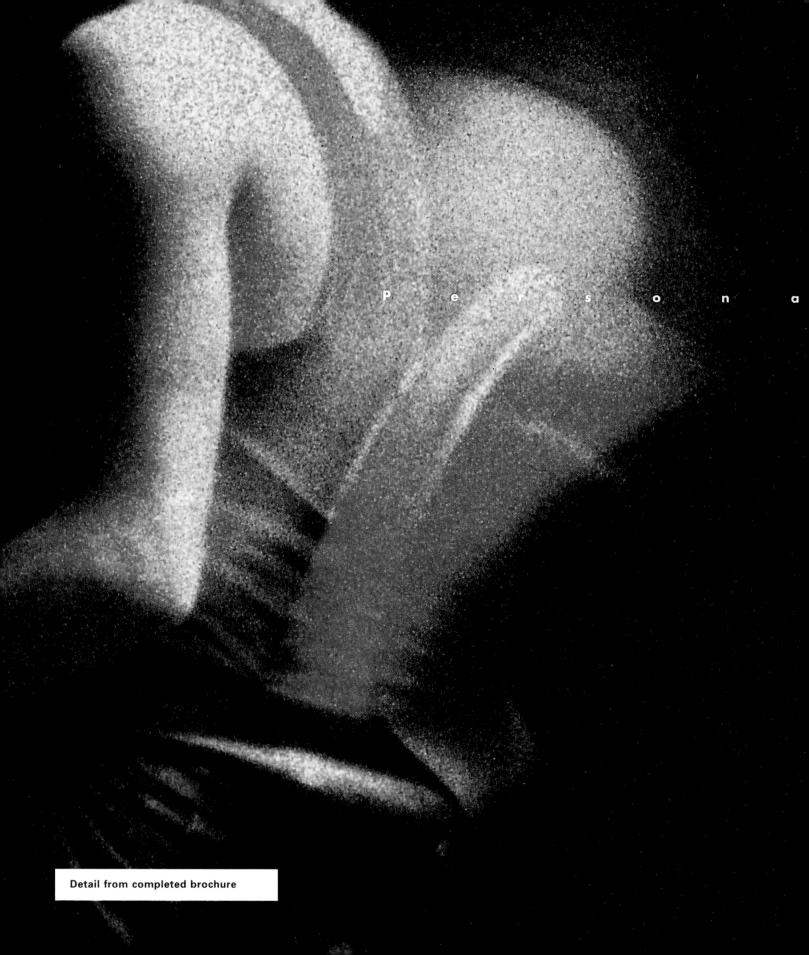

Persona

Detail from completed brochure

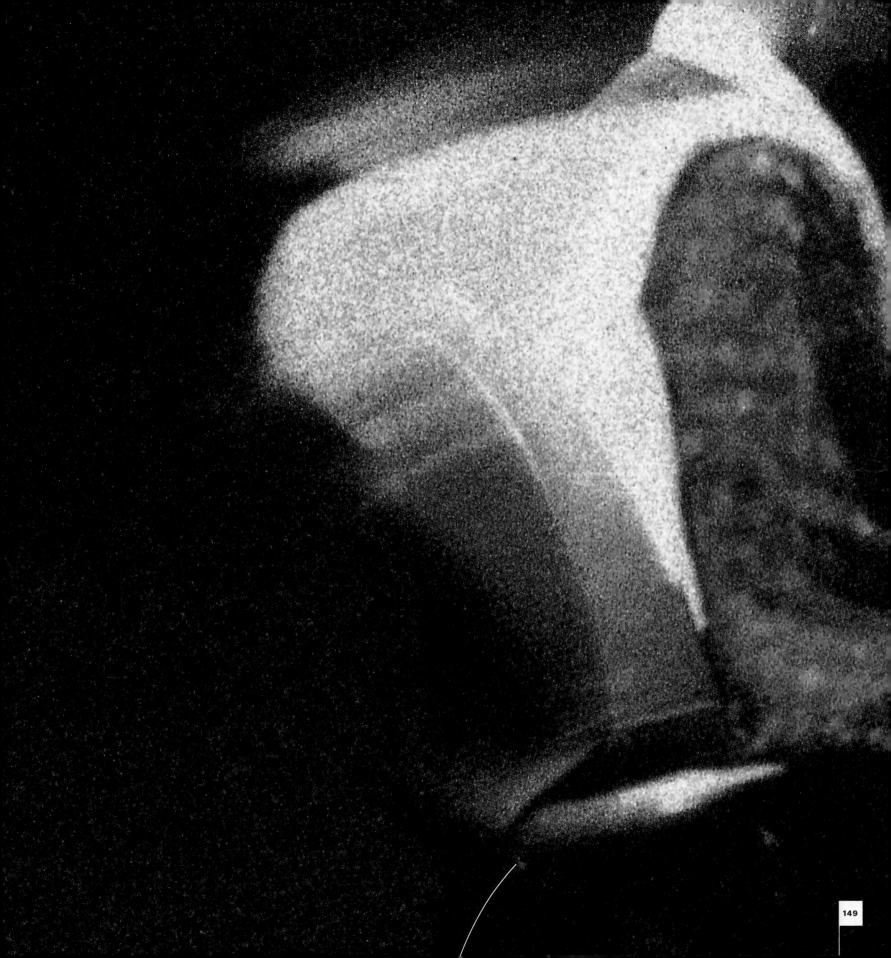

Design for a billboard and poster for the Walker Art Center, announcing an historical exhibition of American graphic design.

The entire billboard / poster is a single Graphic Paintbox collage created at Electric Paint studio in Los Angeles. The source images as well as the main title were entered via a digital laser-scanner onto a nine-track computer tape, from tape to disk, then layered and edited using Paintbox tools. The completed com-position was then passed through a recently added Hell computer for final pre-press and color control. The resulting image was converted into a 4"x 5" color transparency from which conventional separations were made, or, in the case of the billboard, output to disk for computerized giant enlargement.

My concept was to create the image of a single American flag from a composite of historical reproduction techniques:

The texture of each segment reflects the tool that made it, from left to right: sharp line and stipple, steel engraving; a pattern of colored dots, four-color offset; a blurry horizontal raster, video; a mosaic of unique "pixels," the digital computer.

GRAPHIC D

Steel engraving

Offset lithography

Video

**Photography
(prior to computer
manipulation)**

SIGN IN AMERICA

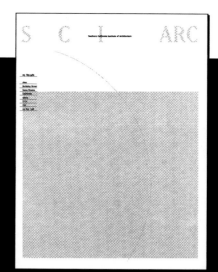
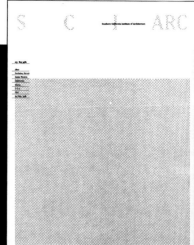

Graphic System for SCI-ARC

A work in progress for the Southern California Institute of Architecture.

The SCI–ARC logotype uses a modified version of the Macintosh font, Emigre Matrix, chosen for its merging of "architectural," classical, and computer-generated qualities.

SCI–ARC, a growing school, requires a great diversity of materials in a wide variety of formats. The goal of this program is to provide a graphic approach, together with computer templates, rather than a complete, fixed system. Since the Macintosh is already integrated into SCI–ARC classrooms and offices, the studio will simply help SCI–ARC staff to decide the ways in which this modular kit of graphic guidelines may flex to suit new needs. In a sense, users will become part of the design process.

Library of letterhead possibilities

S C I — ARC

S C I ARC

Southern California Institute of Architecture

213 829 3482

1800
Berkeley Street
Santa Monica
California
90404
USA
FAX
213 829 7518

One of the final versions of the letterhead

SCI–ARC admissions brochure

Identity program for SCI–ARC, the Southern California Institute of Architecture.

SCI–ARC is "on the leading edge of design practice," a school in which "faculty and students are challenged to engage in cross-disciplinary exchanges." As the first printed piece a prospective student might see, I wanted the admissions brochure to represent the school's remarkable, innovative approach to the teaching of architecture.

The brochure is printed on translucent vellum, layered and ambiguous in its relationship between two and three dimensions. The inevitable print-through on this paper stock is part of the visual texture of each side. The horizontal photograph (in a clay-green) is a multiple exposure of a studio class improvisation, shot directly from the proof

sheet. It is printed as a conventional halftone (one panel, a subtle computer scan, is an exception).

The brochure uses both Matrix and Univers typefaces. The overall texture of names in Day-Glo orange on the reverse side lists recent visitors to the school. Body type is black; "SCI–ARC" is in a 10% screen of black.

Printed brochure

Scanned version of photograph

19 89

Acknowledgments

The works in this book speak for the evolution of my studio over a thirteen year period. At first it was just myself, an assistant, and a part-time bookkeeper. Now it's a group of ten plus, and much more work. At the same time, I'm actively involved in everything we produce and continue to stress experiment, the exploration of new tools, and the expression of a personal agenda as our reason for being.

When I began, I was my own part-time production person. Eventually, with a few more bodies and the incorporation of video and computer technology, the studio has evolved into a more complex organism. I am still the chief designer. I still meet with the clients, define the problem and, with them, develop the concept. I still create the initial sketch using my Stabilo pencil, Prismacolors, or the computer, then hand it off to the assistant who will continue to develop it with me.

At this point I suggest the direction of the project, encouraging alternate approaches. This contradictory process does not always go smoothly. Egos hang in the balance, time is lost, there is tension between studio as school and studio as profession. I am frequently away, and work can bottleneck. My habit of feeling my way toward a solution can confuse rather than clarify. More often, though, the result is a unique collaboration and a feeling of strong collective energy.

Many people have contributed to my progress, especially my teachers at the Basel Kunstgewerbeschule, Armin Hofmann and Wolfgang Weingart. A perfect contrast: the intense, quiet, reductive approach of Hofmann and the additive, complex, emotional approach of Weingart. I was impressed that in Hofmann's class one could study a single detail for half a year, while in Weingart's class you might be working on twenty variations on a single theme at the same time. And a special acknowledgment to Dorothe Hofmann for introducing me to the pencil!

I would like to extend my heartfelt appreciation to my current core staff: Todd Hays, Elizabeth Bain, David Hutchins, Lyn Bradley, Muriel Smith, and Michael Ellison. Michael deserves a special mention for inspired designing under constant pressure for the past three years, this book included. Special thanks are due Paintbox virtuoso and friend, Bob Engelsiepen, and my prior family of principal assistants over the last several years: Michael Giammanco, Ron Romero, Karlee Green-Swift, and Claire Dishman.

My thanks also extend to the "Big Boys" in the profession for their encouragement, advice, or a simple squeeze: Massimo Vignelli, Milton Glaser, Saul Bass, Colin Forbes, and Ivan Chermayeff. They used to be skeptical. And to my personal mentors, Jayme Odgers (hand / eye / spirit), Eric Martin (mind / technology / spirit), and Kurt Sickert (body / earth / spirit).

I am especially fortunate in possessing enlightened clients — Mildred Friedman, Rolf Fehlbaum, Robert Fitzpatrick, Barton Myers, Michael Rotondi, Linda Peck, Lynda Weinman, Alexander Jacobsen, Douglas Schmidt, Shi Yu Chen, and Akbar Alijamshid.

And to other professionals with whom I have collaborated, consulted, or found inspiration — Deborah Sussman, Paul Prejza, Harry Marks, Michael Peters, Michael Vanderbyl, Tak Igarashi, Michael Cronan, Izzika Gaon, Robert Brown, Susan Reinhold, Katrin Adam, Keith Godard, Tom Ingalls, Harold Huttas, Richard Hoppe, Marvin Zweier, Vernon Simpson, Silvija Zemjanis-Wolf, Paul Hinckley, Angeles Arrien, Edith Sullwold, Margaret Fitzgerald, John and Margaret Coy, Don Bartels, Nancy Smith, Barry Kaye, Constance Haft, and Bruce Halperin.

And to those whose contributions are too varied to describe but too important to omit — Kim Haggin, Wendy Drapanas, Phillippe Apeloig, Tony Redhead, Ilene Nakada, Claudia Alberts, Cheri Gray, Noreen Morioka, Deborah Brochstein, Robert Jensen, Steven Silvestri, Clara Pollini, Enrico Boettcher, Zvend Quiroja, Margo Willits, and Andreas Kemmerling.

Credits

Photography	Raul Vega, 15
	Steve Kahn, 33
	Jayme Odgers, 16, 17, 18, 19, 25, 26, 29, 31, 35, 39
	Paolo Utimpergher, 78
	Claire Dishman, 46, 47
	Michael Ellison, 52, 83, 86, 101, 116, 117, 119, 123, 124, 126, 127
	Kurt Sickert, 66 (original photo), 104, 105
	Tom Bonner, 96 (original photo)
	Enrico Boettcher, 138
	Tom Vack / Corinne Pfister, 147 (original photos)
	Ron Romero, 87
	Anthony Caldwell, 155
Videography	Claire Dishman, 48
	Eric Martin, 60

Index

It is important to have a secret, a premonition of things unknown.

It fills life with something impersonal, a numinosum.

— Carl G. Jung